THE

SEVEN PAPERS

REVISITED

CRITICISMS AND CLARIFICATIONS

An Interview with Subhuti
by
Jyotika

THE SEVEN PAPERS REVISITED: CRITICISMS AND CLARIFICATIONS

© Jyotika and Subhuti 2023

1st edition September 2023

ISBN 9798862117325

Front Cover Image: Stupa at Maes Gwyn, built by Subhuti

Published by Triratna InHouse Publications
www.triratna-inhouse-publications.org

TRIRATNA
INHOUSE
PUBLICATIONS

Contents

FORWARD

Over the course of a number of weeks at the end of 2018 and beginning of 2019, I interviewed Subhuti about the *Seven Papers*, which largely consist of written discussions he had with Bhante Sangharakshita about ten years previously.

The publication of the *Seven Papers* was warmly welcomed by many in Triratna, who appreciated the clarity and direction they provided after a turbulent period in our history. Other people, however, were critical of them, claiming they were prescriptive, rigid and an attempt at institutional overreach.

I was intrigued by the extremity of the responses. After some initial research, it became apparent to me that the majority of critical responses to the *Papers* were not concerned with Doctrine: they were concerned, instead, with what it means to be in a Buddhist spiritual community in the present day, and, more specifically, what it means to be part of the Triratna Buddhist Order and Community. I asked Subhuti if I could interview him about it - he agreed, and the following publication emerged from this.

It's over four years since I interviewed him. Shortly after compiling and editing the material, the mother and father of unexpected events - Covid - intervened, and I put the interview in a drawer. Other events kept it there, but now I've dusted it off and, with Lokabandhu's generous help, I'm making it available to those who may be interested in it. Subhuti says there are certain points he would make somewhat differently now but is happy, overall, for it to be published as is.

Many thanks to Vidyadevi for proof-reading and helping to edit it, to Lokabandhu for publishing it, and to Subhuti for engaging so fully and openly with the questions I asked.

Jyotika

Dublin, August 2023

ORIGINS AND OVERVIEW

"Without some sense of this – (the interaction between what lies beyond the conditioned and the conditioned itself) – in whatever terms one wishes to speak, I'm not sure our Order is sustainable, especially in the light of the criticisms of Bhante and his history and personality."

Subhuti

JYOTIKA: Can you explain a little about the origins of the *Papers*?

SUBHUTI: The title, *Seven Papers,* was rather accidental. The papers that make up the *Seven Papers* each had an independent origin, and were gathered together in one volume by Dharmachari Lokabandhu entirely on his own initiative in 2013. As far as I remember, he didn't consult me about the contents or the publication of the book; and I should stress, that I see no reason why he should have. Although there is clearly an internal connection between the papers, they were never conceived as constituting a whole or as pursuing a broad common agenda.

The *Papers* began in 2009 with *What is the Western Buddhist Order?* This came towards the end of a period of turbulence in the Order consequent upon discussion of Bhante's sexual activity in the past. Bhante himself had had a long period of illness during which he knew very little of what was going on in the Order. In 2000 he had formally handed on the Headship of the Order to the College of Public Preceptors. In 2004, I gave a talk at an Order Convention in which I said that I thought 'Headship of the Order' was not an appropriate term for the position that Public Preceptors held, but this statement, and others I made in the talk, inadvertently created a lot of confusion. What I meant was reasonably clear: I was talking about the different kinds of decision-making processes involved in our community, dividing them into three categories – Preceptors' College, Order, and Centres and other movement institutions. In each case, responsibility for making decisions rests with different collections of people, according to different principles and processes. In effect, I was saying that I didn't think Public Preceptors could make decisions on behalf of the Order, and in that sense could not be considered as 'Head of the Order'. I didn't see what I said as especially revolutionary, but it had far larger implications than I had intended and caused considerable confusion.

Difficult as it was at the time, exploring Bhante's sexual past, his illness, handing on the Headship and what that meant needed to be debated, and still needs to be and probably always will. Naturally, many of us were interested in what Bhante's take on these discussions was, and took the opportunity to discuss it with him as he emerged from his long and painful period of illness. He suggested that some of us meet with him and discuss these questions, recording what was said, then editing and publishing it. As I remember, there was no prepared set of questions or even an especially clear idea of what we wanted to talk about, but pretty quickly the question of what the Order was arose, and Bhante gave his view of it.

First of all he asserted that, in effect, it was he who could define what the Order was, and referred to it as the community of his disciples and disciples of disciples, practising in accordance with his particular presentation of the Dharma. Of course, since then the term 'disciple' has come in for discussion, and Bhante has clarified what he means, without insisting anybody use the term. But that definition of the Order was not one that had ever been made explicit before.

JYOTIKA: Another phrase, 'a re-founding of the Order', emerged from the paper, *What is the Western Buddhist Order?* It also needed clarifying, which Bhante did in his short piece, *Rainbows in the Sky*. In this he writes, "when I spoke of a re-founding of the Order, what I had in mind was a reaffirmation of the principles and ideals for which we stand and for which we have stood from the beginning. If one can speak of a re-founding at all it can only be in the sense of making the original foundation stronger."

Could you say a little more about this? 'Re-founding the Order' is a dramatic phrase. What was it attempting to communicate?

SUBHUTI: The phrase was Bhante's. It was meant metaphorically rather than literally. His defining our Order "as the community of my disciples and the disciples of my disciples...and so on" in *What is the Western Buddhist Order?* made explicit for the first time what, as far as I was concerned, was always implicit; that is what the Order has always been. I doubt if I would have said anything exactly like that before, but that is the way it was for most of us, probably until about the Guardian article in 1997, which raised, for some people, serious questions about Bhante's place in things. I can't say how widely people ordained in the early 2000's were aware of Bhante's particular place, but there certainly were some who came into the Order without sharing this perspective. Since it had never been made explicit or clear, then it is understandable that they might not think in those terms.

That then is what I understand as the 're-founding' to constitute: a making explicit what the Order implicitly had always been. Bhante performed all the ordinations until 1985, and from then to 1990 all ordinations were done on his behalf, if not by him. Those to whom he handed on responsibility for conducting ordinations were themselves ordained by him, and carried out their responsibilities appointed by him to do so. The ordination ceremony is imbued with a unique understanding of spiritual life in the spiritual community. Bhante explained in *What is the Western Buddhist Order?* that he had simply performed a function that others had done before him in Buddhist history: re-expressing the Dharma for his disciples in relevant terms and building the institutions of a new spiritual community. Sangha, of course, exists on the highest level as the Arya sangha, and it exists on the broadest scale as the Maha sangha, but individual Buddhist practitioners need to belong to a particular sangha if their Dharma practices are to truly deepen and fructify. The function Bhante performed was the establishment of a particular sangha, within the larger Maha sangha and inspired by the ideal Arya or Bodhisattva sangha. In *What is the Western Buddhist Order?* he stated the nature of our sangha in a way he had not done before, but which was completely consistent with what had been implied all the way through. That is what re-founding meant in that context.

I am aware that for some people this statement about the Order in 2009 was something of a shock. For some ordained in earlier periods, a sense of distance had grown with Bhante and some had lost confidence in him because of what they perceived as his unskilfulness, while others were never really fully connected with him, especially those ordained in the early years of the 21st-century. Having had my own struggles in coming to terms with Bhante's personality and activities, I can sympathise with those who find this difficult. However, I doubt if there is any real basis for an Order without a recognition of the points that Bhante made, however one might choose to express that, avoiding problematic words like 'disciple'. The 're-founding' consisted merely in an explicit restatement of what had been implicit from the start, and that restatement, with suitable footnotes and commentary, is, I believe, still the basis of the Order and the one on which the Public Preceptors' College carries out its responsibilities.

JYOTIKA: Ok. So we have *What is the Western Buddhist Order?* What came next?

SUBHUTI: From that emerged *Revering and Relying Upon the Dharma*. The initial impetus for this paper arose from discussions Sagaramati and I had been having over a number of years. We were both concerned about the tendency in Bhante's early writing towards capitalised abstraction, usually with a rather Hegelian ring: the Absolute, the Transcendental, the Unconditioned. Sagaramati, especially, was concerned that these could easily be interpreted as suggesting a sort of neo-Vedantic eternalism: a reality that lay behind the world of appearances. We talked about this quite extensively and decided that we'd like to engage with Bhante about it and see what he had to say. For me, there was an issue that lay within that issue: I wanted to be clear what view Bhante espoused and on the basis of which he'd established our System of Practice. I discussed all these points with Bhante and he suggested that I interview him. He didn't feel he could easily unfold his thoughts if there was more than one interlocutor, especially because he could not make notes or easily see the people he was talking to. It, therefore, fell to me to have these discussions, which proved to be one of the highlights of my life. Over several days I engaged him in conversation about matters to do with the Dharma. Though my own role was pretty much that of my famous namesake's interventions in the *Diamond Sutra*, nonetheless I felt I was engaged with a dynamic dialogue of a very high order, and that our two minds were very closely attuned.

Fairly early on in the discussion, Bhante addressed the apparent discrepancy between some of his earlier modes of presentation and his later. At that time I was relaying to him the concern that Sagaramati and I had that his earlier language had, at times, tended to suggest a kind of eternalism. So he suggested the hermeneutic principle (that being a principle of interpretation) that his earlier writings should be interpreted in the light of his later ones.

JYOTIKA: Some people have understood this to mean that his later presentation of the Dharma, in particular the *Seven Papers*, supersedes his earlier writings or teachings. Is this what was meant?

SUBHUTI: No. He didn't mean that his earlier teachings were now obsolete and that the later teachings were the gold standard. There is an astonishing consistency from the earliest phase of his teaching right the way through to the present. Interpreting his earlier teachings means exactly what it says: what Bhante said in the past should be read in the light of what was said more recently, which can amplify, deepen and very occasionally correct.

JYOTIKA: How was *Revering and Relying Upon the Dharma* received?

SUBHUTI: Overall, very well: people appreciated Bhante's perspective on the Dharma being brought into sharper focus. Some, though, believed they were being told what to think but I was never really able to understand it as prescriptive. I only saw it as a way for Bhante to clarify certain key aspects of his teaching when he could not do so himself, given his being partially sighted and rather infirm. I presumed that Order members would want to know what the founder of our Order thought about these very important questions. As Bhante said in, *What is the Western Buddhist Order?* he does not expect people simply to accept whatever he says but he does expect them to take him seriously.

JYOTIKA: We won't go through the origins of each paper in detail but could you give an overview of their provenance?

SUBHUTI: After I'd written *Revering and Relying Upon the Dharma*, I had no thought of writing anything further. But I received feedback stating that the paper only dealt with the more metaphysical side of the Dharma and this led me to think that there was more to be said, especially concerning imagination, which Bhante says takes off when reason can go no further. From this, came the paper, *Re-imagining the Buddha*.

Similarly, after I'd finished this paper, I had no thought of anything further. However, after a while, I realised there was more to say about the sadhanas that we took at ordination and their relationship to the traditional Tibetan view of initiation. Once again, I had some conversations with Bhante, rather shorter this time, in which I clarified with him the status of the practices that were taken at ordination and their relationship to the act of Going for Refuge. He made it clear that ordination meant commitment to a broad range of practice, and that ordination was an initiation into that broad range. We then discussed the horizontal dimension to the four stages of the System of Meditation, with the fifth element of Just Sitting.

All of this I wrote up in a new paper, *Initiation into a New Life*. Here I tried to set forth the way in which ordination is the key point in an Order member's spiritual life, and that all other aspects and stages are implied within it. Although nothing very new was said, I was able to draw out themes that had not been mentioned before, especially the Five Aspects of Spiritual Life and the addition to the four stages of the System of Meditation of the stage of Spiritual Receptivity, which corresponded to the practice of Just Sitting. Once again, this had been implied in Bhante's teaching over the years but had never been drawn out. It made clearer and more explicit what Bhante's System of Meditation was and how that was the basis of our Order's practice. Once again I checked all this with Bhante and he endorsed it, particularly recommending it to Private Preceptors.

And again, I thought I had no more to say. But I had a further series of exchanges with Bhante during which I picked up on his very strong sense that there is a dimension to his experience that is not at all explained by 'personality'. Throughout our discussions, I'd had a sense of him hinting at something working in the universe as well as working through him that was of the greatest importance in understanding our Order. Although discussing this is very problematic because of the eternalistic ring to the language and ideas one is forced to use, in terms of actual experience I think it cannot be avoided. The rather narrow and rationalistic language that is often used to describe Insight leaves something unexplained, something unexpressed in the actual experience and that itself is misleading: nihilism is in some ways a greater danger than eternalism.

Leaving aside *What is the Western Buddhist Order?* it seemed to me that if one took the three papers I'd written up to that point as a kind of sequence, the first paper, *Revering and Relying Upon the Dharma*, guarded against the dangers of eternalism, *Re-imagining the Buddha* explored the faculty of Imagination in Dharma life, thereby giving a more positive content to the lived experience, and the description of the place of ordination in the total system of the Order, in *Initiation into a New Life*, helped to flesh out how that more positive dimension expressed itself. However, that dimension itself still required exploration, so I picked up on Bhante's language of 'a supra-personal force' and explored that in my fourth paper, '*A supra-personal force or energy working through me': The Triratna Buddhist Community and the Stream of the Dharma*', to give it its full title.

JYOTIKA: Given its eternalistic ring, is 'a supra-personal force' not destined to be misused and misinterpreted?

SUBHUTI: I have been a little alarmed at the ease with which people on one side have started to use the language and idea in a literalistic, even jargonized, way, and on the other by how readily people dismiss it, again from a literal interpretation without looking at its poetic resonances. That is the problem of all discussion about the interaction between what lies beyond the conditioned and the conditioned itself, as represented in ordinary human beings. However, I think it is important to set this forth. Without some sense of this, in whatever terms one wishes to speak, I'm not sure our Order is sustainable, especially in the light of the criticisms of Bhante and his history or personality.

I also wanted to make clear the place of our institutional life together as a manifestation of this 'supra-personal force'. To me it seems that our membership of an Order has to have a practical outcome in terms of our action together in the world – in terms of a movement. I wanted to make a case for that at a time when so many issues and assumptions about our Order and movement had become much more complex.

So, once again, I got Bhante's approval and endorsement for what I'd written.

After this paper, I didn't believe there was anything further to be said in that sort of vein and I have not felt drawn to explore anything further. I do, however, have some more material – like on the subject of astral planes! – from the remarkable set of conversations I had with Bhante that I've not made public but I would like to do so at some point.

Another of the papers, *The Dhamma Revolution and the New Society*, began as a pair of talks I gave at an event in Padmaloka that were very kindly transcribed by Dharmachari Akuppa, and then edited into a single paper by me. My purpose in the giving the talks, and then publishing them as a paper, was to try to clarify the relationship between Dr Ambedkar's vision of political and social transformation on the basis of the Dhamma and Bhante's ideas about the development of the institutions of the movement. Though I'm sure there's much more to be said, I think I fleshed out the broad principles.

Generally speaking, with the *Papers*, I did what I set out to do, which was principally to clarify in my own mind key issues connected with the Order by exploring them with Bhante, and then writing them up. Of course, it all happened at a particular time in the life of our Order and movement and wasn't without some relationship to the issues that were current. However, I did not write it with those issues in mind, at least certainly not at the forefront of my mind. This may seem a little surprising but it is not the way I work. For better or worse, the processes seemed to unfold within me, if not independently of, but not primarily provoked by, external discussions and debates. I did not have a kind of mental 'hit-list' that I was gradually ticking off as I challenged the various critics who might be making their points at any particular time. I was striving for a deeper understanding and reflection. I still feel fairly satisfied that I managed. I know there are many holes in what I wrote and much room for misunderstanding.

The *Seven Papers*, of course, contains another paper: *A Buddhist Manifesto*. This had a quite separate origin and purpose, although it appeared around the same time as the other papers. Bhante had for some time been saying that he thought we needed a clear statement of the principles of our Order, especially for other Buddhists. I found this far harder to get to grips with, especially as earlier attempts met with rather stinging rejection from one old friend. But my mind tends to organisation and the making of concise statements, so in the end I found the writing very engaging and fruitful, even if it is not particularly poetic or inspirational in style. For me, inspiration often comes in the form of conceptual clarity, but I'm aware that this is by no means to everybody's taste.

With *A Buddhist Manifesto* my principal help was Dhammarati who saved me from my own follies in many cases and helped me to clarify yet further.

Once I had a finished version, Bhante went through it and gave it his approval, preparing a Preface for it, recommending it to other Buddhists and the Order. His hope was that it would be distributed widely in the Buddhist world, though unfortunately this has not really happened. Dhammarati did take a pile of them to a European Buddhist Union Teachers' Conference and was delighted to find that quite a number of those who read it were very much in sympathy with what we set out. Even some of the Theravadan Bhikkshus, though they could not agree with Bhante's conception of sangha, found themselves in close accord with many of the other principles. It really does seem that the Buddhist world, at least in the West, is catching up with where Bhante was fifty years before.

A number of Order members responded to the *Manifesto* by saying that while they approved of the overall character of the booklet it didn't give a positive account of family life. There is something in this and at some point in the future I'd like to revise the work with this in mind. (*Editor's Note: these changes have subsequently been made. See, https://adhisthana.org/a-buddhist-manifesto/*)

So this is how the *Seven Papers* came about. As I hope is clear, it was much more ad hoc, informal and unpremeditated than their appearance in a single volume might suggest.

JYOTIKA: There is a sort of eighth paper, *Buddhophany*.

SUBHUTI: That was a short enunciation of principles behind the practice of sadhana that Bhante published himself, and was included by Lokabandhu in his book. It wasn't a paper, more a distillation of material covered in *An Initiation into a New Life*.

TRANSITIONS

"...some people felt the Papers were tablets of stone they were being hit over the head with, but that's just the way my mind works, it just tries to get things clear. My attempt is to get it understood, not to make it palatable"

Subhuti

JYOTIKA: You've spoken privately about a transition from an ever-present Bhante in the early days who was in the midst of so much – all ordinations, developing his teaching via expositions of Dharmic texts and how they relate to Western culture, etc – to his eventual withdrawal during the nineties. When this happened, it appears that the set of principles upon which our Order and community stand – what you call our common framework of understanding – was not collectively clear. Was he aware of this at the time?

SUBHUTI: I'm not sure, but I had been on at him for some time about this area, more from confusion than clarity, and I felt it just wasn't clear what we distinctively were. With some men who were training for Ordination, I found myself veering between thinking in terms of, "oh he is very sincere and dedicated but is sort of doing his own thing, with his own practices – so should that stop him being an Order member?" while on the other hand having a very tight understanding of what an Order member was. So Bhante had never articulated the principles that allowed the Order to grow from a relatively small group of personal disciples to a much larger group of disciples of disciples etc. But it seemed to me that as we grew and personal communication with Bhante became more difficult because of increasing numbers, we needed greater clarity about principles as well as clearly articulated systems.

JYOTIKA: So there has been this major re-orientation from Bhante at the epicentre of activities to his withdrawal and our basing ourselves on principles. A lot of Order members, who came into the Order when Bhante was at the epicentre, and those who came in before the principles were clearly articulated i.e. pre-the *Papers*, had to make a shift to engage with it when the principles did get articulated, and that transition was always going to be a challenge for some. On top of this, the dialogues you had with Bhante were so fertile and gave rise to so much material that many people felt overwhelmed by them; they weren't expecting them and experienced them, especially given their volume, as oppressive.

So with the *Seven Papers* a lot was being asked of Order members and many weren't prepared for it, and the amount of material exacerbated an already difficult situation for them. It's been a big transition for the Order: some made it early and easily, others are perhaps still in a process, and there are those who have rejected it and the *Papers*. So for those who have rejected it, but still feel their heart is in the Order, what would you say to them? How would you try to get them to think of the *Papers* in a different, more positive way?

SUBHUTI: The first thing I should say in response to that is I was trying to get things clear for myself. I wanted to engage with Bhante to make a contribution but as much as anything I wanted clarity myself. I felt a lot had got very loose and vague, especially in the meltdown years after Bhante's illness and Yashomitra's letter etc., during which time I myself went very radical in my thinking at some points. So I wanted to understand where we stood and it was deeply satisfying to me: more than ever before, I got from Bhante what I wanted in terms of understanding, I was able to pursue things in depth in a way that I had not been able to do previously. Bhante also obviously enjoyed and appreciated it.

So the first thing to understand is that one writes to clarify one's own mind. I know some people felt the *Papers* were tablets of stone they were being hit over the head with, but that's just the way my mind works, it just tries to get things clear. My attempt is to get it understood, not to make it palatable, so in some ways I haven't been the right person but I'd understood something more and more deeply and clearly as the interviews for the *Papers* went on, and they began to form a sort of progression. I love to be clear! Sometimes it's a fault but that was what I was trying to do: to get clear about issues that were of fundamental importance to me as a member of the Order, and as a member of the Order with major responsibilities, and I needed to understand what I was engaged with. And it seemed to add up to something that was important to others. I've never been particularly concerned with trying to make it easy – and perhaps this is a fault – rather I've been concerned with trying to make it clear.

During the interviews for the *Papers*, Bhante came out more clearly and firmly than he had before. We also dealt with certain loose elements in the past and Bhante seemed to think the material was important for everybody. So I didn't begin the interviews with the idea that I'd 'sort the Order out'. It really started with me saying to Bhante that I thought he needed to say something about his sex life. We didn't, in the end, start there, instead at some point I said to him I think it's become unclear what the Order is, so we began with *What is the Western Buddhist Order?* And things unfolded from there. The paper, *Revering and Relying on the Dharma,* mainly came out of discussions with Sagaramati. We felt that Bhante's use of philosophical language was, at times, problematic. So it wasn't an attempt to create a political statement. The nearest we came to that was *A Buddhist Manifesto*, but Bhante asked me to write that, primarily, for other Buddhists.

I'm not a very modern sort of writer. I'm philosophically trained to a low degree but my inclinations are along those lines.

JYOTIKA: The *Papers* arose during the period when Bhante had stepped aside and you had stepped down as Chair of the Public Preceptors' College. This period presented the Order with the opportunity to grow and develop, free of your and Bhante's leadership, but that process wasn't allowed to happen because you both stepped back in again via the publication of the *Papers*. Would it not have been better to let the Order have a period of finding its feet without your and Bhante's continued influence?

SUBHUTI: I don't know what the Order finding its feet would've meant. The idea that we could all get together and have a big powwow and come up with what we all agree on is really very, very naïve. The Order has such a wide spread of opinions and attitudes. And what would you have done with the, at that stage, roughly 400 Order members in India? They wouldn't have wanted to ditch or decentralize Bhante. I think it's an entirely naïve idea.

People sometimes use this phrase, 'the Order does this, the Order does that'. But it's only possible to speak of the Order in a collective sense when the third order of consciousness emerges, and that happens only briefly and fleetingly: enough for us to believe we belong to a common Order but not enough that we can say categorically what the Order does or doesn't do as a collective. If Bhante hadn't stepped back in, if you can call it that, I think we would've been done for. I think we would have either become very loose and diffuse with people drifting off or we would've started to form factions and splinter.

JYOTIKA: Maybe we would've been done for if we'd never got greater clarity on our principles but maybe a few years of just letting things unfold, of being receptive, would've helped our sangha and Order integrate the highs and lows that we'd just been through; maybe a period of collective Just Sitting would've done us the world of good?

What I'm grappling with here is an attempt to understand why so many Order members reacted so strongly to *The Papers* and continue to reject them. You've said you couldn't understand why some found them prescriptive. Having spoken with a lot of them, I don't think they've used the word 'prescriptive' - those that have used it – merely in the sense of being told what or what not to do but also in the sense of something pressing down on them, like a restrictive force. And I've been curious as to why they've felt like this.

Back in the early noughties, our sangha was emerging from a period of initial flourishing, of building centres, of developing systems and institutions, like the ordination processes. The ideals of heroism, hard work, sacrifice and self-development, as well as meditation, friendship, study etc., kept the whole thing moving along nicely for a few decades. After the Guardian article, however, and Yashomitra's letter, which triggered a slew of disclosures about the struggles many had gone through as a consequence of things like the heroic ideal and the single-sex idea, we began to question whether a reliance on the path of self-development – of using effort to always improve ourselves – was sufficient for spiritual growth or the gaining of Insight. Generally, it was agreed it wasn't, and from this a much greater emphasis was placed on the phase of Spiritual Receptivity in our System of Practice.

As this was crystallising, as this deeper appreciation for receptivity was settling in, the *Papers* turned up, and they were the last thing many people expected or wanted. By being so clear, so ordered in communicating, amongst other things, the nature and significance of the niyamas and spiral-like conditionality, the *Papers* had, inadvertently, a counter-productive effect for some, who regarded them as a resurgence of an over-focus on the path of self-development and the heroic ideal. And given our history, and new understandings of what had gone on in the past, this was a path and ideal they no longer trusted.

They, instead, were now moving more confidently along the paths of self-surrender and self-discovery, of gaining inspiration from abiding in states of receptivity, of not knowing, of being able to sit equanimously in chaos. Symbolically, the *Papers*, therefore, have represented for them a resurgence that they find oppressive, a resurgence that makes Triratna a community of the 'spirit' - always ascending, in Hillman's usage – with only lip-service being paid to the 'soul', which descends, faces the demonic and is reliant on the faculties of surrender and receptivity. For those who had hoped that our post-Guardian approach would broaden out from a primary focus on the path of self-development, the *Papers* came as a big blow.

I wonder if there is also something about the *Papers* partially colonising, again inadvertently, a mythic or poetic space that had been at the heart of much of what we did, or were, as a community. There are many accounts of the magnetism and strange charisma that Bhante could exude during the late 60's, 70's and 80's: some have described him during this time as conveying a strong sense of 'other', of having a transcendent, mythic dimension, even of the immediacy of ultimate truth. While he was at the epicentre of the Order and movement, this 'other' was a living presence but when he started to withdraw in the 90's, this 'other', inevitably, withdrew too. His withdrawal, plus Yashomitra's letter etc., contributed to something of an identity crisis: who were we? Was Bhante the man we thought he was? What was our common frame of understanding now that he was no longer with us in the way he always had been? And the *Papers* tried to address this thoroughly – especially what our common frame of understanding was – and by virtue of addressing it head on moved, to some extent and however incomprehensibly, into the space left by him. But whereas before that space could be charged with transcendent, poetic transmission, the *Papers* communicated almost exclusively via Reason. And for a lot of people if we were moving from poetry, 'myth' and a tangible sense of 'other' to merely Reason then we were sounding our own spiritual death knell. They, therefore, experienced the *Papers* as a closing down deep within us, and so rejected them firmly and still reject them today.

So, from all this, I have a number of questions:

1) Do you have any sympathy for these experiences and perspectives?

2) Within our common frame of understanding, is the path – or 'myth' as you termed it in your 2003 paper, *Three Myths of the Spiritual Life* – of self-development more important than those of self-surrender and self-discovery?

3) If the *Papers* have colonised, to whatever extent, the space of 'otherness' left by Bhante's absence, is this their rightful place? And if it isn't, where is their rightful place?

SUBHUTI: Is it true that "so many" Order members have reacted "so strongly" to the *Papers*?

JYOTIKA: I haven't done a survey but there are a fair few of them.

SUBHUTI: Well I also know of a fair few who strongly appreciate them. So I'm not sure I can endorse that.

JYOTIKA: Endorse what?

SUBHUTI: That "so many Order members reacted so strongly". I just don't know what the numbers are. You say that, "you've spoken with a lot of them". I'm afraid I think you've seriously exaggerated these numbers and failed to take into account the large numbers who've responded very positively to the *Papers*.

But to respond to your questions: Do I have sympathy with their experiences and perspectives? Only to a degree. I have sympathy with people who can't work out what I mean because intellectual discourse isn't their strong point – I have sympathy with that – but what you've said doesn't seem to me to be anything to do with what the *Papers* are. Most of the criticisms that I've read don't criticise what they're trying to; I think what's behind them is to do with a loss of faith in Bhante.

Then the issue of self-development: what Bhante did in amplifying his discussion on the niyamas was to provide a perspective on conditionality that included all three myths (development, surrender and discovery). The myth of self-development is mainly connected to the notion of karma-niyama; self-surrender, and to an extent self-discovery, come under the heading of Dhamma-niyama because what you are discovering isn't actually yourself, it's a deeper aspect of mind that is more than self. What Bhante referred to, that I fleshed out, was an account of conditionality that provided for all the different myths; it was a real contribution. He had spoken before about the Dhamma-niyama but he hadn't clarified what he meant by it. What he was trying to do was explain why conditionality was the all-embracing, fundamental perspective on the Dhamma in a way that included all the different approaches. In my own practice, this enabled me to put much greater confidence in my deeper experience and my reliance on the Bodhisattva I meditate on because I understood more clearly where it fitted into the overall picture, I understood more clearly the relationship between the karmic (my own effort) and the Dharmic, which was to do with my relaxing and opening-up.

So for me, it's not a conflict between the self-development model and the self-surrender or discovery models at all; the *Papers* provide a unifying perspective. One has to think in terms of karma – as the Buddha did – and one has to think of making an effort to develop skilful states and to move away from unskilful ones: the Four Right Efforts of the Noble Eightfold Path. That can never be done away with until you've completed the Path, even a Stream Entrant can make effort and move more quickly. We can't abandon effort – to do so will be highly problematic – at the same time we need to be aware that there are forces moving within us that are not immediately accessible to our 'will'. The most important function of will in relation to them is to set itself aside. And that is what the *Papers* talk about! It's in *The Supra-Personal Force*. My impression is that some of the critics haven't really read it. Also, the starting point of the second paper, *Re-imagining the Buddha*, was Bhante saying, "where the intellect can go no further, the Imagination must take over".

So if that criticism is being made, that the *Papers* promote the myth of self-development above those of surrender and discovery, then I don't believe the critics are reading them closely enough.

To reply to the question that the *Papers* are overly-rational: there has to be a place for reasonably precise intellectual exposition. A lot of the Pali Canon consists in the Buddha giving intellectually precise communication. It doesn't preclude myth and imagination but it may not include the language of myth and imagination, because that's not its job. Its job, in this context, is to try to tie together a number of points in the light of conditioned co-production as expounded through the niyamas, so that you can understand the fundamental, theoretical framework, you can understand the place of imagination and myth, you can understand the place of Ordination, of where our ceremonial life as Order members is and therefore where our practical life as Order members fits in, and then we can see at the same time that there is something about it all that is not to be defined, as it were, though it can be seen where it fits in. For me, that's all very useful, that we've got an overall perspective in which one can understand all the different aspects of things. For instance, I drew out from Bhante the Five Aspects of Spiritual Life that give you a way of understanding the different teachings and a framework into which we can look at new teachings and practices and fit them in. The need for imagination and myth does not preclude the need for intellectual precision. I think one of the most useful things in the *Papers* was my defining the safeguards of imagination, because imagination without clarity is madness or genius but a genius of a kind that leads to mania and religious fundamentalism. So intellectual clarity is essential. There has to be a clear View! Tibetan Buddhism – so mythically rich – is profoundly concerned with View. The *Papers* were never an attempt to communicate fundamental truths of the Dhamma via different modes of expression: myth, intellect, emotion etc. That wasn't what they tried to do.

I'm astonished people have made this type of criticism of the *Papers*. It's not as if they reject the intellect: their attacks, on the whole, are intellectual! It seems as if the *Papers* aren't being read with sympathy and a sense that something is being communicated in them that's important. I suspect they've attacked the *Papers* mainly because they believe they're being told what to think. And this comes down to their relationship with Bhante, and perhaps to some extent with me.

JYOTIKA: You've said that the language of the *Papers* is the language of the niyamas. This model includes spiral-like conditionality, and presumably moving towards and onto this mode of conditionality is the goal, but does it not over-emphasis what Hillman terms the 'spirit' - always ascending – as opposed to the 'soul'?

SUBHUTI: I've no doubt that Mr. Hillman would've been far too intelligent to critique Bhante's presentation of the Dharma as being merely about 'spirit'. I'm sympathetic to his model but you must be very careful not to read one system in terms of another. Hillman's is to do with the psyche in relation to wholeness; the *Papers* are to do with processes of conditionality. For instance, a lot of what Hillman talks about comes under the heading of Integration; and it's worth remembering that Bhante talks not only of horizontal and vertical integration but also that there is vertical above and vertical below. You can't make spiral progress until you've a fair degree of integration, both horizontally and vertically.

I think what we actually see in our Order and movement is that there has been a process of maturation, but this is something critics of us often miss out. We were a bunch of twenty year olds with a guy in his forties who'd returned from India at a time of extraordinary cultural turmoil. And we were younger even than our years because of the huge cultural change that was taking place. If I'd been born ten years earlier, I would've matured within the system of my parents but that system didn't work anymore. So the models for maturation had weakened or gone, thank goodness I'd say. We were young people who hadn't had the benefit or the curse of traditional society to help us grow up and so were therefore unusually susceptible and unbalanced. And then there was this man who was exploring how to communicate the Dharma in this new setting, and to his very great credit, for which undying gratitude should be paid him, was willing to experiment and explore. Some of it was messy, even harmful, which was really regrettable, but it was so fundamentally right that gradually, through our engagement with it, we've reached a new maturity. Yes, we need to acknowledge the mistakes, the harm, but you have to see it in a larger perspective. I'm not sure its possible to bring the Dhamma into a cultural setting that was in such a state of flux and not have some false starts. You look at all the Buddhist groups who began at that time – they all made mistakes. But through the process of engagement, through Bhante's willingness to learn and our willingness to practice, I believe we've achieved a degree of maturity that we should give ourselves credit for. It's not possible to set up a perfect Order; it's why there was a Vinaya.

JYOTIKA: I'm still trying to understand the perception that seems to be out there that the *Papers* strongly endorse the paths of development, reason and heroism above other approaches, with people struggling to relate to them and instead feeling much more comfortable and drawn to teachers and retreats that are orientated towards the myths of surrender and discovery.

SUBHUTI: But each of us has a different way of communicating, and in different contexts, I can communicate very differently.

JYOTIKA: Of course but here I'm interested in the perception. Bhante had withdrawn from the epicentre during the nineties, then retreated quite dramatically from public engagements for a few years from 2003. You, yourself, went into a long retreat in 2008. And then it was like you both re-emerged, perhaps re-invigorated, back into public view, and the *Papers* began appearing. And this re-emergence – largely publically via highly crafted rational expositions of the Dharma, ie the *Papers* – gave the impression that you were both determined to communicate that the paths of self-development, heroism and reason were the pre-eminent ones. Perhaps it was merely a question of timing: there had been an absence, when the Order began looking at itself in a different way, then a sudden return to Bhante and you at the epicentre, publically at least, with all this material.

SUBHUTI: Look, without ethics, without effort and without karma, self-surrender leads to madness and self-discovery leads to self-obsession. It's the rationally expressed framework that is at least some guarantee against that. If you wish to surrender, what is it you are surrendering to? If you are discovering, how are you to be clear that what you are discovering isn't just a post-modern indulgence into a fantasy of yourself? I think this is a very real danger. If there are no wrong views, you don't need reason, but how can you have no wrong views this side of Enlightenment? Wrong views are rampant. There needs to be a clear exposition of Right View. This was the purpose of the *Papers*. This clear view then enables an approach to myth and the deepening of experience that is unproblematic.

Having said that, I do have a sense of what you are talking about but a number of issues are getting conflated and confused here. As you've introduced it, I'll use Hillman's model to illustrate my point. Moving from 'spirit' to 'soul' is part of the process of integration and maturation, and young people tend to 'spirit' - they are idealistic, dreamers, followers of visions of a better world or life (and this is an essential phase) – but as they get older they need more 'soul', they need to learn to navigate the often treacherous waters of practical living as well as to be with the whole of themselves, that which isn't inspired or visionary etc. This movement from 'spirit' to 'soul' can also be experienced within a community as a whole, and it's one I believe our Order and movement has gone through; we have matured, we're not the bunch of twenty-somethings we once were, liable to institute misinterpretations of Bhante's teachings.

The purpose of the *Papers* was to articulate Right View and a common framework of understanding upon which the principles of our Sangha could be based. They weren't a resurgence of 'spirit', to use that language, or a regression back into an immature state; to see them that way is to fundamentally misunderstand them.

Some critics of the *Papers,* however, seem to me to be motivated primarily by institutional and personal reactions. If they don't like the *Papers* then they should forget them; let those who like them take them on. What I'm told is that young people find them really helpful otherwise they get so bewildered by all the different approaches that are out there. But I think some people, some Order members, have lost the idea of an Order. They've got an idea of a loose affiliation of people who've got a long association together but who are principally exploring on their own. That's not the Order; it's not our central vision. I believe they've lost a fundamental faith in Bhante and thereby have lost the unifying perspective that we share.

JYOTIKA: If after reading this, someone feels like re-engaging with the *Papers*, where's a good place to start?

SUBHUTI: I think the best place to start is with *An Initiation into a New Life*. It marks a crossroads in the *Papers'* sequence, and is crucial in that sense: *Revering and Relying Upon the Dharma* and *Re-imagining the Buddha* build up to it, and the *Supra-Personal Force* takes on from there. So to my mind that's the key one, more especially as it ties the *Papers* back to ordination.

CULT OF PERSONALITY

*"I think there is inevitably a tension between those in the Order
and movement who have a reverence for Bhante, verging on the
cultic, and those who dismiss or devalue him, verging on the
cynical. But I also think there's an acceptable middle ground,
containing less extreme versions of both of those, within which most
of the Order is functioning healthily"*

Subhuti

JYOTIKA: In 2009 Bhante, in *What is the Western Buddhist
Order?*, defined the Order, "as the community of my disciples and
the disciples of my disciples ... and so on."

In April 2017, he stated in *'A Note on 'Discipleship'* that

"The Triratna Buddhist Order is a ... Sangha of those who share
my understanding of the Dharma and follow practices that flow from
that understanding ... I have come to think that no single term,
including 'disciple', can adequately define all those who share my
understanding of the Dharma and follow practices that flow from
that understanding."

And,

"It is necessary for all Buddhists that we feel an emotional
connection with and sense of gratitude towards those from whom we
have learned the Dharma teachings that we follow. This is more
especially the case in relation to those whose understanding is the
basis of the Sangha to which we belong. It is therefore important that
all Order members feel such a relationship with me as well as, in the
case of those I have not ordained personally, their own preceptors."

I'd like to begin this section by asking a general question about the Guru/Disciple, Preceptor/Preceptee relationship as it's, obviously, an extremely rich and important one, yet rare in nearly all cultures in which the Triratna community operates.

Do you think, as a sangha, we do this type of relationship well?

SUBHUTI: It's very difficult to answer because what is the standard? And how do we combine all the different kinds of relationships and see whether they've been done well or not?

Nonetheless, I'd say we don't do it badly, as a whole.

JYOTIKA: How would you distinguish between a traditional Tibetan Guru/Disciple relationship and a Triratna Preceptor/Preceptee one?

SUBHUTI: The most straightforward answer is that in the Guru/Disciple relationship there is an element of ritualised deference that can be quite artificial. I once went with a young Tibetan to see a very prominent Rimpoche. When we arrived my Tibetan friend prostrated himself fully three times at the feet of the Guru. I then had a conversation with the Rimpoche, whom I wasn't especially impressed with; he didn't really seem willing to engage in genuine communication – perhaps he was having an off day. Afterwards, my Tibetan friend spoke very disparagingly of him. So, you had that extreme deference and that cynical dismissal running side-by-side. I think essentially that the Tibetans, or certainly that Tibetan, viewed the Guru as a sort of archetype separate from the personality of the individual. I hope we don't do that in Triratna. I hope that where there is genuine appreciation, and even reverence, that it is on a human basis, though projection is almost inevitable at some stage.

JYOTIKA: To suggest that Order members should feel an emotional connection with, and gratitude for, Bhante and if he has not ordained them then with their Preceptors as well, has been criticised as an attempt to institutionalise a cult of personality around him. On the other side of the spectrum, many Order members feel a profound reverence for him, and most, if not all, of us, at least during Ordination training, have spent or spend time bowing or prostrating regularly to his image on a shrine. We have, thus, as a community, a tension between those devoted to Bhante and those who feel a certain respect for him or who are generally critical of him. The latter can claim the former's devotion to be naïve and mindless, while the former can accuse the latter of being individualistic and counter-dependant.

So do we have a cult of personality around Bhante? And is it possible to close the gap and ease the tension between those who revere him and those who merely respect him or are critical of him?

SUBHUTI: First of all, one would have to define a cult of personality. It seems that the term rose to prominence in post-Stalinist Russia, and was used in a critical way of Stalin by Khrushchev. What is implied is the according to a particular person of quasi-divine status, someone who cannot be questioned and whose every action is assumed to be in some sense perfect or at least deeply meaningful. The cult of personality is sustained by conscious, or semiconscious, effort by the manipulation of media, via its various platforms, so that the image of the individual in question is inflated in people's minds. One of the commonest characteristics of a cult of personality is the unwillingness of followers to criticise or even to question the object of the cult. When people do question or criticise there will be a strong reaction from the cult members and indeed from the 'authorities'.

So then, do we have a cult of personality around Bhante?

Obviously, we do not, certainly in the sense in which the term is usually used. It is possible to question Bhante and many people have. It is possible to disagree with him and many people have. It is possible, even, to believe that Bhante has acted wrongly or said things that have had harmful effects – and quite a lot of people think he has.

I think there is inevitably a tension between those in the Order and movement who have a reverence for Bhante, verging on the cultic, and those who dismiss or devalue him, verging on the cynical. But I also think there's an acceptable middle ground, containing less extreme versions of both of those, within which most of the Order is functioning healthily. It's partly a matter of temperament, partly a matter of age. I've certainly had times when I've assumed that everything Bhante did was motivated from the highest possible level: and I've had times when I've considered him to be a rather ordinary man getting his own way in a not very exalted fashion. I would say these days my own perspective is somewhere in that middle ground: I have very great gratitude to Bhante and a feeling of reverence for him, at the same time as recognising that he has a personality and that personality has sometimes imprinted itself too strongly upon the Order and movement, largely not as Bhante himself would've wished. In other words, I don't think he wanted to be the centre of a cult.

JYOTIKA: The founder of the Rajneesh movement, Osho, established it around the centre of his personality, and his followers see him as having divine status. If Bhante didn't want this type of structure or relational dynamic within Triratna, what is at our centre?

SUBHUTI: Rajneesh/Osho is certainly presented as all-knowing and all-wise. Although I've had little contact with anybody from that movement more recently, I have had over the years. Everything depends upon Rajneesh and every word that drops from his mouth is perfect. It is not possible to discuss him as anything other than an Enlightened Buddha. To their credit, Osho followers used not to mind if you didn't think that – they tended to have a somewhat tolerant attitude, though underlain by a definite sense of superiority. Rajneesh, himself, definitely cultivated this idea of himself, which Bhante very definitely has not done. Indeed, I would say that he has gone out of his way not to. What we have at our centre is the Buddha, Dharma and Sangha as Refuges, not Bhante. We don't even see Bhante in terms of the fourth Refuge of Tibetan Buddhism, by and large, and certainly not as part of official doctrine.

It must also be said that, especially in the last few years, there has even been an 'official' acknowledgement that Bhante's actions have caused harm and even been unskillful; though this has been, justifiably, carefully worded. Indeed, as far back as 2003, in a talk I gave to a Men's Order Weekend, which was widely distributed, I publicly acknowledged, as Chair of the College of Public Preceptors at the time, that I thought Bhante had done wrong in his sexual behaviour.

JYOTIKA: But has that been enough? David Cameron, when Prime Minister of the UK, apologised on behalf of the British people for the wrongs of Bloody Sunday in Northern Ireland. This was forty years after the event yet his apology had a profoundly healing affect on the Catholic community who suffered so much that day. Obviously, I'm taking a very extreme example, and perhaps it's unfair to even associate it with our situation, but I'm doing so to highlight how an acknowledgement of specific wrongdoing years later by someone who wasn't personally involved but who held the seat of leadership of the people involved healed so much. Where the comparison with our community could come in, is that no-one in authority in Triratna has really stood up on behalf of the community and apologised for specific wrong-doings, sexual or otherwise, in our past in which people got hurt. It could be argued that Bhante's apology in, *A Personal Statement*, 2016, did this. But his apology was so general in nature and needed two further clarifications in 2017, one in February, another in November, which for some merely increased the sense of acting on the back foot and offering too little, too late.

There was also, as you say, the 'official' acknowledgement but was this too carefully worded? Do we not, as a community, need someone, ideally the Chair of the Public Preceptors' College, to stand up and reach out publically to those adversely effected by Bhante's actions or those of others in authority by simply acknowledging their pain and saying that, on behalf of Triratna, they are sorry it happened? Would the symbolism of this not have a very healing affect, not only on those who suffered but on our community as a whole?

SUBHUTI: I'm afraid to say that your thinking here is woolly. It is unfair to compare our situation with the events of Bloody Sunday and its aftermath. Apologising within the context of an institution is complex, and the type of institution makes it more complex still. Within the institution that is the British Government, the principle of monarchy rests upon the idea of continuity of authority, and that is still the mythic legal framework of the British system: The King is Dead, Long Live the King. So David Cameron, as Prime Minister, can apologise on behalf of the British government for any action taken at any time in its name. However, the same does not apply within a spiritual community such as ours. Within a spiritual community, the principle is of individual responsibility; only I can take responsibility for my own actions or failure of action. This is very important. We can express regret that something happened within our sangha but we can't apologise or confess on someone else's behalf.

So far as I'm concerned, the College of Public Preceptors have reached out, and are reaching out, to those affected by what happened in the past. Saddhaloka issued a letter on behalf of the College to all Order members in March 2017, in which he states, "*We will actively seek to resolve any harm that has been done, using the principles of the Dharma, with outside experienced guidance where appropriate*". And true to its word, the College has been following up with anybody they know of who may have felt unhappy with their sexual contact with Bhante; and some have taken them up on this, some have not.

As well as this, they have made it very clear that they do not think there should be sex between Preceptors and those they ordain, and support the Triratna Ethics Kula's ethical guidelines that prohibit sex between teachers and those they teach.

I think if the Public Preceptors go any further than this, alongside doing what they can to resolve matters with anybody who's been affected, then they'll distort the sangha and turn it into something other than a Buddhist spiritual community.

JYOTIKA: Ok. We digressed there from our primary theme. To return to it: what's wrong with a cult of personality?

SUBHUTI: The problem with a cult of personality is that it encourages dishonesty and lack of individuality. That is, of course, if one understands cult of personality in its full-blown sense as outlined above. A cult of personality distracts from the truth and does not allow differences and a real sense of personal responsibility.

JYOTIKA: If we don't have one now, could we have one in the future?

SUBHUTI: I doubt if a cult of personality can develop in Triratna. One cannot, of course, predict everything about the future, but I think it is extremely unlikely. This is partly because of Bhante's own way of thinking and talking and teaching. He's definitely spoken against anything that might be considered a cult of personality. It's also because of the strong emphasis on individuality and on honest and open communication, that are very much characteristic of the movement overall. If a cult of personality does develop after his death, it would have to be able to take into account what has emerged about his sexual activity. Whilst I do not think that Bhante's sexual activity was motivated by predatory lustfulness, it's obvious that he judged poorly, at times; at least it appears so in hindsight.

For a cult of personality to develop in Triratna in the future there would have to be a mythologising of aspects of Bhante's history that are now very much part of the public record. Unless there is a radical transformation of society and culture, it won't be possible to suppress this. Therefore, a cult of personality would have to take into account what happened by giving it a positive spin and adding it to the cult of personality. I think this is so unlikely that it is not worth considering. We no longer live in times when things could be easily forgotten or suppressed. I suppose the only circumstances under which a cult of personality could develop in the future would be were

Triratna became allied to a repressive state that managed to control the media. Naturally, I do not think this would be a good thing.

Of course, whilst I don't think a cult of personality would be a good thing at all, and that it would mean the betrayal of what is essential about Triratna, I think that a proper acknowledgement of our debt to Bhante and appropriate feelings of gratitude and respect are essential to the future.

JYOTIKA: As the language and experience of Insight deepens within our community and discourse, do you see a danger that cults of personality around other Order members might develop in the future? And how might we avoid this?

SUBHUTI: Yes, indeed I do see a tendency or a potential at least, for a cult of personality to develop around people who are seen by others as having some sort of attainment. This is a conundrum left to us by the Buddhist tradition: the Buddha gained Insight, gained Bodhi, and many of his immediate disciples seem to have done so too, therefore this is an ever-present possibility with serious practice of the Dhamma. Furthermore, the Buddha actively recognised a number of his disciples as having gained various levels of Insight, up to and including Arhatva. The problem is that if people lay claims to attainment they are laying claim to a certain infallibility of understanding of the Dhamma. Of course, in reality, it's not as simple as that. However, it is almost inevitable that claims to Insight will lead to a certain degree of adulation from the credulous, which is probably most people when it comes down to it!

I remember Bhante being asked once if he had Insight. He responded saying, "if I say I have, how would you know whether to believe me or not; if I say I haven't, what difference would it make to your practice of what I teach you?" I think this says it all.

JYOTIKA: But some people would say that if he doesn't, then his teachings aren't to be completely trusted, that they wouldn't have full confidence in him.

SUBHUTI: But that means that they are relying on 'authority', not the Dhamma itself or their own experience. I remember him saying to me years ago that we've all got some Insight. He didn't see Insight as such an absolute thing. In his response to the question 'does he have Insight', he's exhorting his interlocutor to rely upon the Dhamma and to rely upon himself - don't rely upon me.

On the other hand, I remember Viryabodhi told me that he asked Bhante if he was a Stream Entrant. Bhante responded simply by saying, 'it's important to have confidence in your teacher'! But your confidence in your teacher needs to come from your confidence in your experience of him or her, rather than from your belief that they have a certain attainment or accolade. This is my concern with the language of attainment, it means that I stop focusing on what you say, on what sense it makes to me and how I experience it in my actual practice and so on, and I start relying on it as 'authority'.

If Bhante's refusal to say that he has Insight weakens a person's confidence in him then I'd try to get the person to look at where and how they place their confidence.

JYOTIKA: Schopenhauer's philosophy was criticized on the basis that he himself, as a man, didn't measure up to it. Schopenhauer in turn dismissed this by saying his role as a philosopher was to chart and point the way, while it was up to other saintly beings to traverse it. It's slightly different with Bhante, but there is something of that flavour in what he's saying, isn't there?

SUBHUTI: Yes. The Kalama Sutta says that just because a teacher says, "I have attained", don't accept it. What is important is when you yourself know these things are true and lead to happiness etc. So I think that was what Bhante was getting at. And we can have such a literal idea of Insight, as if it's a sudden big moment and everything is different. Maybe it is for some but I don't think that is necessarily the case.

On the whole, however, I think issues that arise from declarations of attainment are generally self-correcting in a sangha such as ours;

although some will be taken in, most will not, which will then result either in people singly or in groups leaving the Order or in the gradual setting aside of the claims and returning to normal, humble, serviceable membership.

I think where we have seen in the past the dangers of a cult of personality are more in the organisational and leadership field. We have seen, and still see, a number of people in outstanding leadership positions who have become somewhat isolated from their peers and unassailable in their position: nobody can question them because they have such respect for them and because they have such dominance. This is why we strongly encourage 'term limits'. This prevents a slightly unwholesome symbiotic relationship developing between leaders and those in their Centres or activities.

I believe this is simply a reflection of a general phenomenon that has been observed, for instance, in business and especially social activist groups. It's even come to have a name, 'Founder's Syndrome': it's called that because it most often afflicts those who start organisations, build them around themselves, and become almost inseparable from the organisation and difficult for others to dislodge. Our whole system within the Order and movement, with its various safeguards and multidirectional intersecting bodies, should guard against this. It's most common where somebody has gone off by themselves and set something up, but it happens from time to time anywhere.

Having said that, we also want to make sure that concerns about the excessive dominance of individual personalities does not mean that we do not allow very strong and confident people to function. It should be possible for outstanding individuals, in any field, to express themselves, flourish and take a lead without everything becoming overly focused upon them. The main point is, of course, that they should be in contact with their peers and kalyana mitras, and should be very regularly in positions where they have no position. Having found myself in something of this position, although not very extremely I hope, I know what it's like from both sides.

REVERENCE

"There are definitely things about Bhante that I disapprove of; there are things about him that I find difficult; and there are things about him that I just don't find congenial. But what he has done and what he has taught, and what he is, so far as I know it, is far greater than that and invites my deep respect and gratitude."

Subhuti

JYOTIKA: I'd like to explore 'reverence' a little. It's a powerful emotion, deeply embedded in the Buddhist tradition, yet our modern, post-Enlightenment conditioning can make many of us in the West extremely suspicious of it. The English writer Geoff Dyer, writing of the Russian film-maker Tarkovsky, distinguishes between his feelings of reverence for the work of Tarkovsky, as opposed to Tarkovsky the man himself. Could this be a useful distinction to make, especially for Westerners, i.e. that we feel reverence for Bhante's work as opposed to the man himself?

SUBHUTI: I don't think this is a useful distinction beyond a certain point. When I see the works of Tarkovsky, for which I feel great reverence, that reverence is essentially for the man from whom the work came. It just doesn't make sense to separate the two. How could I see *Mirror* and be drawn into the deep and subtle exploration of his own experience and then meet the man and just have a chat about football? The work of Tarkovsky is a revelation of Tarkovsky's mind and creative imagination.

Of course, this does not mean that I have great admiration for everything that Tarkovsky did: I'm not sure he was particularly creative in his relationships with women, for instance. A great artist is often not so great in other areas of life. I think we need to be able to revere and feel gratitude for the great and good things people do without giving them blanket approval. I think this is a common misunderstanding, for instance, with the Metta Bhavana, to make an analogy. When you feel metta for your enemy, you are not approving of all the unskilful things the enemy does. You're feeling a deep empathy for them as conscious beings such as yourself, who experiences pain and pleasure and who like the latter and dislike the former. Also, for instance, when you have a friend, you have deep feelings of friendship for them, but that does not mean that you approve of every single action they take: sometimes friendship is taken to mean unconditional support for the friend but I do not think that's what it really means. In a sense, one could say that reverence is metta directed towards someone who's done praiseworthy things or things of real merit. So you can feel your very strong sense of reverence and respect and gratitude without liking everything about them and revering every move they make.

I think this is a very important point. There are definitely things about Bhante that I disapprove of; there are things about him that I find difficult; and there are things about him that I just don't find congenial. But what he has done and what he has taught, and what he is, so far as I know it, is far greater than that and invites my deep respect and gratitude.

I remember when the Guardian revelations emerged in India, a very prominent Order member, who has now left the Order and is a prominent critic, said in a meeting of the Order that 'yes, Bhante did wrong but when you look at the sun you do not point to the tiny sunspots'. The brilliance of the sun's radiance dazzles out those imperfections. Allowing for the rhetorical hyperbole of this image, it is apposite.

Every age has its favourite vices and virtues. Right at the moment, anything to do with a sexual misdemeanour is considered so black that it blots out the sun's radiance. But in another time this would have been barely considered. I'm not saying this is right, I do appreciate and support the attempt to make it much harder for people in positions of power or influence to exploit others, whether sexually or in any other way, but somehow that must be kept in proportion. For instance, I know hardly anything about Harvey Weinstein, apart from the fact that he seems to have used his position as film producer to seduce many actresses. But assuming he was a good film producer, which I'm not in a position to judge, does his extremely unskilful sexual predation mean that one cannot feel appreciation, in some measure at least, for what he enabled? This is, of course, tricky territory.

JYOTIKA: What of Bhante's life and work do you revere?

SUBHUTI: Of course, I cannot give an exhaustive response here. But I think that Bhante has understood in a completely unique way what Sangha is in our times. It is fascinating to see that much more recent Buddhist teachers and leaders are coming to very similar conclusions to Bhante. There's much more that can be said about this but that's the first point.

Then, I think Bhante has understood the principles of the Dhamma in an astonishingly clear and articulate way, and that has enabled us to understand the practice of the Dhamma now, especially as he's linked his presentation of the Dhamma to practices and methods. His ability to get to the heart of the matter excites my reverence and gratitude greatly.

I deeply appreciate Bhante's emphasis on imagination and his weaving into his interpretation of the Dhamma the power of great art and of artistic endeavour, in general. I think it will take many generations for this to be fully revealed but the fact that he's seen it from the start is unique and powerful.

To keep this brief, my final point of admiration, gratitude and reverence is something much harder to put my finger upon. There is present in all Bhante's work, everything he's said, everything he's written, everything he's done, something of another dimension. I've been extremely fortunate, though sometimes it has been difficult, to spend quite a bit of time working closely with him. Even in his darkest times of illness and suffering, I felt directly in him something that cannot be defined merely by his personality. Through Bhante, I felt myself linked to the Dhamma has a living reality. It is this, above all, that I revere in him and I'm deeply grateful to him for sharing it with me and with all of us. I believe that extra something is present in Triratna through him and that if we reject it in him we will have to look for it elsewhere – and who knows if we can find it.

NAVIGATING BETRAYAL

"What I remember in myself during the major reaction that I had about fifteen years ago was the extraordinary confusion I felt as I floundered in my feelings. It was unbearably painful."

Subhuti

JYOTIKA: Though I don't wish to blacken out the sun's radiance by focusing on its spots, I would like to explore the experience of betrayal. Many people within our community have expressed their sense of anger, confusion and disillusionment at Bhante's acknowledged unskillfulness, especially his sexual unskillfulness. The American psychologist, James Hillman, writes that within trust is always the seed of betrayal, and that once we are betrayed in a relationship in which we trusted we could respond in one of a number of ways:

- By seeking revenge
- By denying the value of the person who has been guilty of the betrayal, their ugly 'shadow' suddenly made manifest in place of previous idealizations
- By turning cynical, viewing all 'causes' for fools, all organisations as traps, all hierarchies as evil
- Or by forgiving – and thus entering higher religious experiences.

The resolution of betrayal, for Hillman, is seen as a spiritual/religious issue. However, the ratio of possible negative responses to positive or spiritual is three to one: the odds are not favourable – we are more likely to respond reactively and destructively.

Though we may not have a cult of personality around Bhante, or Preceptors in general, is it not naïve to promote a culture in which all Order members are encouraged to feel, on-goingly, gratitude to him, and to their Preceptors? Is the experience of betrayal not inevitable in such a cultural climate?

SUBHUTI: I'm not sure that we do promote a culture of encouraging Order members to feel ongoing gratitude to Bhante or to their Preceptors. In a certain sense, I don't think you can encourage somebody to feel something. What you can do is make it acceptable to feel it and even to applaud that feeling. This is similar to accepting and applauding the feeling of metta. I certainly don't think we should tell people what they should feel or blame them when they don't, although the fact that they don't may itself require some exploration.

I think a healthy and balanced person can experience gratitude and reverence without any danger of betrayal. Betrayal is after all a betrayal of illusions. One can only feel betrayed by someone in this context if one has expected something of them that they have never offered and that is unrealistic.

My own experience with Bhante illustrates this point. On the whole, I think my reverence of him has been quite clean and wholesome, but there was an element of idealisation and projection, which led to my feeling angry and hurt. But I finally recognised that I'd been taking Bhante as a refuge, and he never offered himself as such nor expected that of me. As I gradually clarified what had gone on, and disentangled my projections from what he is, I was able to respond to him in a much more balanced and healthy way.

Nonetheless, I would say that I think it almost inevitable that considerable numbers of people will, at some period, come across some complication in their relationship with Bhante or other kalyana mitras or Preceptors. I think we have a great deal more understanding of this than we did before; during the early days we were still rather naïve. These days if somebody goes through a period of serious reaction I'm not as alarmed as I would have been. I appreciate that something is being worked out, at least in a large number of cases. The main thing is to try to remain understanding and to keep in contact.

JYOTIKA: If we do feel betrayed by Bhante, or by one or both of our Preceptors or Kalyana Mitras, how do we move beyond it and the anger, disgust, cynicism, etc that usually accompanies it?

SUBHUTI: If you do encounter such a strong reaction within yourself to figures you had previously respected and even revered it can be very painful and difficult. The main thing is to stay engaged – although you may not feel like doing so. I have known quite a few people who have broken off contact and then after some time, maybe even many years, come back having resolved matters, having a deep appreciation but without illusions. But I can't think of any prescribed way in which this unfolds.

What I remember in myself during the major reaction that I had about fifteen years ago was the extraordinary confusion I felt as I floundered in my feelings. It was unbearably painful. I remember the resolution for me came in the form of a strong recognition that I had complete faith in the Buddha. I knew absolutely, incontrovertibly, that he was Enlightened and that he did teach the Dharma. It's as if I'd landed on absolutely solid ground. Gradually, everything else took its place. I realised that I had developed that deep inner certainty about the Buddha through Bhante. Everything I knew and experienced about the Buddha came to me through him, more or less directly. The problem was I'd got the Buddha and Bhante mixed up. The emblem of the resolution came in doing the Prostration Practice. There was the Refuge Tree in front of me with the Buddha at its centre. On the lotus stemming towards me sat Bhante and his teachers, between me and the Buddha. It seemed to me that I was Going for Refuge to the Buddha through Bhante: it was he who had introduced me to the Buddha as he really is. From that point on I was able to accept the things about Bhante that I'd been reacting to, which were in a sense real issues. I can accept that they were as they were but that they did not alter what Bhante had given me. What a wonderful relief.

I think what happens when you feel betrayed is that your illusions get shattered and because one's faith is all of a bundle the whole thing breaks up. You need to take the space and time to get it all disentangled. And other people need to give you that space.

In my own case, once the dust settled, I realised what I owed Bhante. This wasn't something I had to think out, it was something that simply was there. What I am, certainly what I am for the best, was largely because of him. Even the context in which we can have sometimes difficult and painful discussion is because of his conception of sangha. It's interesting to note that a number of other groups who have had their own difficulties with their past have admired our way of going about it.

JYOTIKA: It is said that, "to understand all is to forgive all", but some people claim that the problems caused by Bhante's unskillfulness were so grave, and have become so culturally systematic, that to simply forgive him is not an appropriate response, it is too simplistic and overlooks the wider difficulties it's caused. What's your response to this? Do you believe Bhante is worthy of forgiveness?

SUBHUTI: I don't think there is a question of Bhante or anybody being 'worthy' of forgiveness. Forgiveness is unconditional: if you really do understand, then you really do forgive. Indeed, you can forgive somebody even when they are unrepentant. However, I do not think this is the case with Bhante. All I can really say is that I do not think that the problems of Bhante's unskillfulness were so grave and culturally systemic that we have to do anything more than we've already done in relation to them as a community.

I think it is a good thing, though difficult, that there has been a general sense that the past is open to full examination. I think much useful reconciliation has already taken place. I'm not myself completely confident, however, the truth has really emerged. This is not to say that I think there are new dark shadows to be revealed. What I'm getting at is that the truth is not just to do with bad things that happen. After all, in those early days we were living at a time of great cultural confusion and a huge opening up in so many areas of life: sexual, gender, relations with authority etc, they were all coming up for reassessment. The old religious certainties were finally collapsing. In that gigantic bonfire of the past a new world was forged. In a certain sense, we didn't know what we were doing. But look what has been created, even in the midst of our naïve confusion. I don't think the real truth can emerge in a climate of recrimination; we must get beyond that. I think it will take another generation for it to happen. For instance, I've never really told my story!

JYOTIKA: As a way of rounding off this section, what lessons have you learned, both as a Preceptor and Preceptee, that, if you could go back in time, you'd share with your younger self?

SUBHUTI: As a Preceptor I wish I had realised how complicated the relationship can be because the Preceptee is often working all sorts of things out in relation to the Preceptor. In other words, there is a fair amount of projection or even transference. For instance, I have recognised, rather later than I should have done, that young men often need to find their feet independently of older and more senior figures. I can't speak for young women but no doubt it's pretty much the same. Sometimes I've been quite hurt by what is obviously a necessary process of disentangling this entanglement of the 'junior' party from the 'senior'.

What I have learned in my life in general, and wish my younger Preceptorial self had known, is that one should be very careful with giving advice. Even giving advice about spiritual practice should be done with great caution. One's main contribution is to help people to clarify themselves to themselves and to work out for themselves what is best for them to do. Naturally, helping to bring about that clarification does bring to bear one's own experience, which is a sort of guidance, but it should not be prescriptive.

Another thing I've learnt is that there are many twists and turns in spiritual life and that what seem like reactions can simply be necessary processes of clarification. I wish I'd been able to recognise earlier that someone was going through a phase rather than thinking they were lost to the cause.

On a similar note, I would say that I've learned to recognise that other people are often very different to me. This means that what I say about myself does not necessarily easily apply to them.

Whilst I've not had too many disasters in my career as a Preceptor, most of the difficulties I've had could have been avoided by these sorts of reflections. Whether or not I could have heard them if my older self told me them at the time I rather doubt. I think one could sum up a lot of the points above by speaking of the need not to get at all possessive in a Preceptorial relationship, not to feel that one's own well-being is tied up with the successes or failures, however one comes to judge those, of one's Preceptee.

Much of what I've said about being a Preceptor applies to being a Preceptee. It took me quite a while to 'grow up' to Bhante, at least in human terms. But again, I doubt if it would have been possible to listen to this advice at the time.

WHEN THE GROUND GOES FROM BENEATH US

"you need to let people go, let them feel it's understandable that they're disillusioned or whatever, and to remain in dialogue with them as much as you can. This can be difficult. When someone you've invested quite a bit of love and care and attention on turns around and smashes you it can be hard, but there you go, you've just got to take it."

Subhuti

JYOTIKA: Order members can reach a point in their lives when old certainties vanish and an existential and spiritual re-orientation needs to take place, when they need to inhabit a non-identifiable zone, which is often a very painful place, where they feel no particular allegiance, no particular loyalty, no desire to identify as anything, and yet they don't want to leave the Order. They may, during this period, feel deeply critical of the Order and angry with individuals they once admired. This experience, for some, could belong to the 'Death' phase of our System of Practice. Inexperience, over-idealisation and the grasping onto dreams as opposed to truths, inevitably, condition much of the early part of our spiritual life; as we mature this reaching into the wrong places begins to weaken and break down. And this breaking down can, and probably will, be messy.

How do we as an Order support Order members who may be having this experience, which may result in them engaging in harsh criticisms of individuals in the Order and the Order as a whole on social media or in Shabda?

SUBHUTI: I thoroughly agree with you, these phases do go on, though I'm not sure I'd put them under the heading of Spiritual Death, I'd say that it's more a psychological process, it's a question of growing up, of not putting trust in the wrong thing or person. So, like I said earlier, I got the Buddha and Bhante mixed up. And I think that was largely to do with my relationship to authority in my early life. I don't put that down to being real Spiritual Death, though it is part of that process.

JYOTIKA: So how would you characterize a Spiritual Death experience?

SUBHUTI: It's when you really see how your ego-identity is constructed and is not ultimately real. And from this, you begin to become genuinely selfless. In ordinary karmic life, there can be little deaths, where you've had illusions about yourself and life, you've projected onto others etc and you suddenly realise it's not true, it's all empty and the whole thing collapses. These experiences are very important but they are of a different order to a Spiritual Death.

JYOTIKA: But they're necessary stages?

SUBHUTI: Yes, especially because of the nature of our western culture in which we can be so 'conscious', and not everyone is raised in a loving home. You don't really get this in India, where children are really loved, by and large, so you don't get the same breakdown and anger and betrayal and so forth in later life that you get in the West. Indians don't do the radical disillusionment that Westerns can do; I've hardly seen it there. Perhaps this is to a fault, but I think it's from a much stronger sense of community, and of being raised, generally, within the context of a loving and extended family.

Just to go back to your original question, I think the relationship of the individual to the group and the individual to the spiritual community is inevitably fraught with problems, and it will for some people lead to a significant crisis, where they lose all sense of their identity and belonging. The main thing is for key figures like teachers, Preceptors and kalyana mitras to understand that this may happen and not be too worried about it. Here the issue can be that sometimes one builds one's hopes on people, which I think is something every parent knows, that they live out their own expectations through their children, and to some extent one can end up living out one's own expectations of the spiritual life through the people one is kalyana mitra to. So you need to let people go, let them feel it's understandable that they're disillusioned or whatever, and to remain in dialogue with them as much as you can. This can be difficult. When someone you've invested quite a bit of love and care and attention in turns around and smashes you it can be hard, but there you go, you've just got to take it.

JYOTIKA: Why do you emphasize not worrying too much about it?

SUBHUTI: Well, if someone decides they don't want to go on in the Order, they don't want to follow the path as you think they should, just let them go. Things often work in very odd and unforeseen ways. You just don't know how it's going to unfold. I've come to believe something I'd never have said before, but that simple, ordinary life is sometimes the best conditions for people to grow.

JYOTIKA: Does that mean moving out of the sphere of the Order and movement?

SUBHUTI: I think sometimes, yes. I wouldn't necessarily encourage someone to do it but if they wanted to, and were clear about why they wanted to, then I wouldn't oppose it.

It can be very easy to have expectations of people, but you need to let them live their own spiritual lives. If people do kick at you, you need to try to listen to what they're saying, try to evaluate what's right and what's wrong – it can be a very emotional and irrational period in someone's life but you just have to stick with it.

JYOTIKA: But for how long? Some Order members may experience a re-orientation of their spiritual lives in which they feel no particular allegiance to the Order or are very disillusioned by it, yet are not ready to leave. Presumably, however, it's in no-one's interest for them to remain stuck in this experience. Is there canonical guidance as to at what point a Dharma-farer needs to re-engage positively with his or her sangha or to leave it? And if there isn't a teaching within the canon, do you have a sense of when that point arrives?

SUBHUTI: I can't think of a canonical reference. The classical sanghas were very different, many were monastic for a start, and in traditional societies you don't get the same freedom we have today in the West.

People shouldn't remain in that state of suspension for too long and need to acknowledge a point at which they really have left the Order. I don't think we should force anybody out, and that the Order is going to have to sustain a small minority, perhaps about 5 percent, at times maybe more, maybe less, who are feeling very disillusioned and considering leaving. But I tend to think it rights itself in the end, that at a certain point you find nobody really agrees with you and if you do get sympathy from people its from people who are also disillusioned, and that you are picking through the carcasses rather than on the living whole. Your interests and sympathies will, also, have gone somewhere else. I would hope that will happen, though not with all, some may make themselves a place in the counterculture and get stuck there.

So I have no prescription as to what should happen or how long it should go on for. I would simply say that I don't think it's healthy for it to go on for a very long time: honesty and self reflection will tell you that this has gone on too long and it's time to go. And this has been largely happening.

It's more difficult for those who probably ought to leave but militantly decide to stay. Then it's difficult to feel at ease when they're present. If you're in a gathering of Order members you shouldn't assume collusion is taking place, you should be able to assume a certain level of shared faith and confidence. I've spoken in contexts where I knew some people present were very cynical and critical of what I was saying. I said it anyway but it has an atmospheric effect. Some people have the belief that that's a good thing. But I disagree.

The Seven Strange and Wonderful Things about the Mighty Ocean, from the Udana, comes to mind. The Buddha is sitting with a company monks but says that the company isn't pure so Maudgalyana forcibly ejects those making it so. And there's the analogy of sangha being like a mighty ocean because the ocean washes dead bodies onto the shore, it rejects them, and in the same way the sangha rejects those who are not really in it. So it's like there is a natural process. But some people are stubborn and have doctrines of, "I'm going to stay and change it!" It's part of our contemporary zeitgeist: the hero or heroine on the fringes who stands up and fights.

JYOTIKA: But in a healthy, functioning community or society, we need checks and balances?

SUBHUTI: I agree with that – and there needs to be the possibility of discussing issues – but the Order and movement does not function via the same systems that wider society does. We are a sangha. People can get confused about this, and want to bring in all sorts of different ideas, like those of democracy. I support democracy, and would fight for it and for the right of anybody to say anything, so long as it was not an outright incitement to violence or hatred, but that isn't what a sangha is. For a sangha to operate effectively, there needs to be love, appreciation and a shared sympathy with one another.

INDIVIDUALITY: GLORY OF THE HUMAN REALM?

"We've inherited an idea of an individual as a completely free agent and of us exercising our 'will' in a completely abstract and open way. But we never do."

Subhuti

JYOTIKA: In *What is the Western Buddhist Order?* Bhante rejects the idea that the Order can collectively decide through democratic means what it is, and that as he founded it he decides. This is seen by some as an authoritarian act and contrary to the principle of the Order as being a free association of individuals. Why did Bhante take this position?

SUBHUTI: Because what creates the Order is the witnessing by the Public Preceptor of the Going for Refuge of the Ordainee, and initially that was done by Bhante; he established what that meant in our context. So we've already signed up to what the Order is on that basis, we've already signed up to the fact that it's an Order of those who are ordained in the understanding that Bhante has; whether we thought that through or not, that is actually what we've done. You could argue that if there was a unanimous decision by the Order, in other words by all Order members, to change that then we could do so, but effectively what we'd be doing is leaving this Order and starting a new one.

In terms of a 'free association of individuals', I think people make an issue of that by overextending what it really means. In a certain sense a golf club is a free association of individuals but you're not, as a member of the club, free to turn it into a tiddlywinks club. You freely associate with others not in an abstract sense but in a particular sense.

I think the problem is partly to do with our abstracted notion of individuality that we've inherited from the European Enlightenment. We've inherited an idea of an individual as a completely free agent and of us exercising our 'will' in a completely abstract and open way. But we never do. An individual always exists within space and time, an individual always associates within a particular spatiotemporal context. So the Order is of a particular kind in which we freely associate with each other on that basis. Of course we are completely at liberty to freely disassociate ourselves and freely associate elsewhere. It is by a voluntary act that you accept the ordination, which is symbolized in the Ordination ceremony by the request. So I think the statement of the free association of individuals has been grossly over-interpreted from the perspective of an abstracted notion of individuality.

JYOTIKA: So what was Bhante trying to achieve by talking about a free association of individuals?

SUBHUTI: I think he was stressing the notion of individuality, that joining the Order is an active, personal choice, made responsibly: you decide to Go for Refuge within this context. I think he was developing the language of individuality and from the notion of individuality the notion of spiritual community, so you get group, individual, spiritual community. The group is formed of people who are not individuals, who are simply members associating for mutual security, survival and benefit, whereas the individual is one who takes personal responsibility for their own moral action. The spiritual community consists of individuals who freely associate with each other under no compulsion.

JYOTIKA: That is the ideal, of course, whereas in reality ...

SUBHUTI: It's not always so clear cut.

JYOTIKA: Exactly. Notions of individuality in the West, especially since psychoanalysis and Jung, include things like wholeness, independence of mind and the emancipation of oneself from the herd. This cultural conditioning lends itself to the view that to be devoted to another human being, bar one's lover or children or, at a stretch, an infirm parent, is a weakness, a testament of one's sub-individuality. Do you believe there is truth to this? And is it possible to be a true individual while feeling devotion to Bhante or one's Preceptor?

SUBHUTI: To me it all depends on what you mean by 'devoted'. What Sangharakshita has taught us is that the issue is psychological dependence. In other words, if you are emotionally dependent on the other person for approval, love, security etc, that is definitely sub-individual. For him, indeed, devotion to one's lover or rather dependence on one's lover is the primary mode of such sub-individuality that we encounter. In this state of dependence, one is unable to assert one's own thoughts and wishes in the face of fear of loss of love or approval or security. This is certainly understandable but ignoble.

However, that does not exhaust the possibilities of human relationship, otherwise we would end up, all of us, completely isolated from each other. It is possible to have a fully individual devotion to another. In other words, you are full of metta for that other, which may include even some sense of their superior qualities or at least of strong gratitude for what they have done.

It is if we have two extremes: one where one's own individuality is subordinated to another, while on the other one is completely isolated and cut off from others and cannot enter into positive relations. The notion of maitri in Buddhism encompasses friendship and kalyana mitrata, both the vertical – in both directions, up and down – and horizontal kinds. When kalyana mitrata is really kalyana mitrata there is no sense of dependence. Each party is fully an individual but linked in a loving and creative mutual communication.

I remember the great shock I got when studying Milerepa's last meeting with Rechungpa with Bhante. Rechungpa leaves for India, despite Milerepa's wishes for him to stay, and Milerepa watches him wind his way down into the valley towards the plains of India and weeps. When his lay disciples come, they are very anxious and concerned and ask why he's crying. Milerepa simply says, "Rechungpa, my heart son, is leaving and I shall never see him again". I remember immediately being struck by the contrast with all the Arahats around the Buddha at his Parinirvana, none of whom shed a tear; it was only Ananda who wept, but then he wasn't an Arahat! Did this then mean that Milerepa's attainment was less? Bhante's explanation was that every true friendship brings about new creative possibilities and anyone who has truly creative energy will definitely recognise the ending of that possibility. This made a deep impression on me, and I saw that spiritual development did not mean an increasing isolation and self-sufficiency in a narrow sense but a deepening of human connection beyond mere dependence. I should say that I think that this is probably present to some extent in what otherwise might appear as dependent relationships. One sometimes senses that people who have been married to each other for a very long time have gone beyond the merely dependent element in their relationship and something more like a depth of friendship has developed. A characteristic of that would be a non-exclusivity.

So, in sum, I'd say that if you were a true individual you would feel deep devotion and gratitude to those who have played the kind of important part in your spiritual life that Bhante has for me, and Preceptors can for others. There's a famous story that is not found in the Pali Canon but in a later tradition: the Buddha, in the second week after his Enlightenment, stood gazing at the Bodhi Tree with deep gratitude.

JYOTIKA: Recently when you were in Hungary, you had another way of talking about social consciousness that wasn't in terms of the group, individual and spiritual community. Could you say a little about that?

SUBHUTI: This is from the angle of awareness rather than a sociological category. There is a way of seeing the world as a group member in which you look for those who belong to your group and who you therefore consider will provide you with security, survival and will work with you against others. And it's literally true. I found as an Englishman being there with an English woman, Danasamudra, in Hungary that I felt, at a more instinctive level, a kind of bond with her. That wasn't everything that was going on but I noticed it was there. I also noticed the way in which gypsies tended to see other gypsies and non-gypsies. And everybody does in one way or another, as soon as you're in a social situation you look for those who are going to support and protect you and work with you to your mutual advantage, and you look for the indicators, the flags that they wave. It's a mode of consciousness that is essentially based upon the survival instinct of the individual organism. 'Individual' consciousness is a shift so that you see the world from the point of view of moral, aesthetic and spiritual values. You look at the world from that perspective and those values. They may, at times, conflict with your survival interests and the more of an individual you are the more you are willing to stand up for them. There was a striking example of this recently that I saw on the news where a Sikh policeman in India waded into a Hindu mob, at considerable personal risk, that was trying to lynch a Muslim. Someone had taken a picture of him and he was obviously really frightened but he has this Muslim and is shuffling him out of the crowd. He said afterwards that was his moral duty, as a policeman or not, to save another human being. That is a high level of individuality at the cost of possibly his own life, certainly his own comfort and safety; he was willing to stand up for the value of life. That's the mark of individuality – that you stand upon values. Sangha consciousness is where you, as an individual, sense the same values in others and as a consequence of sensing those values in others are able to let go of your personal attachments and clinging and enter into a mode of consciousness that is quasi-telepathic. So it's a way in which the world appears to you. I found that particularly compelling.

JYOTIKA: Presumably all three modes of consciousness can manifest in the one moment, and depending on conditions will manifest? In terms of the group, the individual and the sangha, the group has been thought of as the antithesis of the sangha and individual, and therefore dangerous to both. In this model, the group has no merit, yet we all inhabit it from time to time. Perhaps when we think of 'free association of individuals' we assume that we've transcended the group, whereas in your 'social consciousness' model that's never really going to happen.

SUBHUTI: I think you could say that true individuality emerges only with Stream Entry, but even at Stream Entry, famously, greed and hatred still manifest even though you don't give them free rein, and these drives are essentially to do with personal survival and are, therefore, going to be affecting your attitude to others and will entail a certain amount of group consciousness. I think group consciousness is far deeper than we realise: it's far more basic and essential.

The rhetoric that you describe in connection with the group comes from Bhante, "the group is the enemy of the spiritual community", or "the group is always wrong", "the individual is always right", all that sort of thing. The purpose of it was to appeal to us to be individuals. Because we were the generation that was revolting against the past, it was very attractive to us. I think Bhante slightly liked the fact that it was attractive to us, which was not a bad thing. But he did also talk about the positive group, which in my understanding is a group that is under the influence of values, not because of those values per se but because they're associated with the group's identity. A lot of Ambedkarite Buddhism is group phenomenon but Ambedkar was a considerable individual and stood upon ethical values to a very high degree. So it's part of people's identity to stand for values, which to my mind is a very good thing, even if it can become a bit moralistic and conflictive in a certain way. So I tend to think in terms of the positive group that is accessible to individuality and the spiritual community, and ideally you have a sort of flowing out from the spiritual community into the group to transform the group, first of all into a positive group and then to bring individuals from the positive group into the spiritual community.

It's important to have a more honest recognition of the depth of group consciousness within us, and to think in terms of trying to bring the group into a connection with positive values. I don't use the language of the individual much these days because I think it as been pulled far too much in the direction of individualism, and that plays into a very strong mood in our culture.

CONSERVATION, ALLEGIANCE, COHESION: DIRTY WORDS?

"we have such an individualistic notion of everything, and the whole trend of consumerism, which is accentuated by the Internet...doesn't encourage a strong sense of obligation to a community. But putting your individual needs at the service of the community doesn't mean that anybody needs to lose anything."

Subhuti

JYOTIKA: Bhante, in *What is the Western Buddhist Order?*, stated that,

"within the Order and movement at present ... the loudest voices seem to be in favour of what could be called innovation. I don't hear equally strong and numerous voices being raised in favour of conservation, to call it that. I therefore see that innovation is the current danger, especially in view of the general climate around us and the craze for what is new and different – the new for new's sake."

Bhante said this in 2009, over ten years ago. Since then we've had the publication of the remainder of the *Seven Papers* and time, as a community, to absorb them. Given this, do you think Bhante's perspective and emphasis are still as relevant?

SUBHUTI: I think it will always be relevant to pay attention to conservation, and that the whole tenor of our times is towards the 'new' being better. Our consumerist mentality tends to make us feel that the latest iPhone is the best and a 'must have'. Also, because there's a critical reappraisal of our past recently, the call for something new is strengthened because people have lost confidence, to some extent, in where we've come from, which will tend to mean that they look for somewhere new to go.

So it is still important to stress conservation, but I don't like the terminology of 'conservation'. 'Continuity' would be my preferred word, which I think is the resolution of the dichotomy of conservation and innovation. There needs to be a continuing response to ever-new circumstances because circumstances are ever-new, but that response needs to have continuity – with where we come from and our common basis. To achieve this, I believe we need to have a shared common language, and a shared way of approaching spiritual experience so that we can more easily, more readily, experience spiritual community. That necessitates a strong emphasis on understanding where we come from, the principles from which our understanding emerges, as well as making sure that we continue to practice some things that are continuous with what we've always practiced.

At the same time, there are legitimate grounds for trying to introduce something new, but it mustn't be done on the basis of subjective likes and dislikes, it should only be done with consideration for the community as a whole. When it's done, it must be done because something is definitely missing and because this new thing may supply that need and after we have properly evaluated it and properly fitted into our existing perspective. This area needs to be understood more deeply by some people: there is a coherence to the perspective of a spiritual community and you can't just take something from another perspective and impose it upon the one you have; chances are it just won't fit and there will be all sorts of confusion. An example is the triyana perspective you get in Tibetan Buddhism. Bhante's perspective just cuts through that, it doesn't go there. It was a way the late Indian tradition, inherited by Tibet, dealt with the multiplicity of different teachings; they arranged them in terms of a kind of hierarchy of ascending practice. But it doesn't really work if you look at it very critically and it's not really necessary for us.

So we need to be careful that we don't introduce the language and perspective connected with that into our language and perspective where we don't see things like that, otherwise we'll get confused. Because of Bhante's emphasis on principles, we don't need to do that.

There may be things that we don't have, for instance some people want a more kinaesthetic or ritualistic way of practising, but we don't really have it.

To introduce it requires a careful process of assimilation and consultation, seeing why it's necessary, why what we have isn't enough, and how to ensure it's integrated most effectively.

So, overall, there shouldn't be a presumption that 'new' is better or that we should be actively seeking the 'new'.

JYOTIKA: But many Order members are inspired by many different approaches, and because their inspiration is so alive they want to share it.

SUBHUTI: I completely understand that but I hope people will also have a very high value of the Order and of the needs of the community as a whole. Their personal inspiration needs to be set in the context of the community as a whole. It may be that they simply practice it by themselves and don't promulgate it. Or they feel it's of sufficient importance that's not already supplied and should be considered as a new string to our bow. But people need to reflect on what it takes to have a spiritual community. It's not just an assemblage of people getting on with their practice. A community is a community; it involves putting your individual needs regularly at the service of the community as a whole. But we have such an individualistic notion of everything, and the whole trend of consumerism, which is accentuated by the Internet where there's a huge range of possible interests and rights and so forth, I think it doesn't encourage a strong sense of obligation to a community. But putting your individual needs at the service of the community doesn't mean that anybody needs to lose anything.

But I don't want people to lose their inspiration. What I'd say is that if someone has discovered something 'new' and is in the inspiration stage I'd encourage them to keep it to themselves! When this exciting stage ends and they've got a deeper experience of the practice, then they'll be in a much better position to discuss it with others and see if it's something that's not supplied already and could be of real benefit to the community. Holding a spiritual community such as ours together, which covers different nationalities and cultures, is extremely complex.

JYOTIKA: Which brings us on to the issue of going to other teachers.

Bhante, again in *What is the Western Buddhist Order?* says that,

"In the first place, they [Order members] should affirm that, even though they have taken some teachings from elsewhere, their heart is definitely with me and with the Order and FWBO."

This seems a very important phrase: "their heart is definitely with me and with the Order" and Bhante is, in general, very strong in this paper on loyalty.

I'd like to look at this from another angle. A characteristic of the Western education system is its encouragement of children to be creative, to engage with the arts like painting, playing music, reading stories, especially when young, and to think for themselves. Indeed, originality, individuality and artistic creativity are defining features of Western civilisation. Within this fostering of individual expression, cross-pollination of ideas, styles and perspectives has been essential in maintaining a rich creative ground, and these larger societal forces inevitably shape Triratna in the West. But Bhante strongly discourages Order members from going to other Buddhist teachers, and promotes "narrowness" for the purposes of achieving depth. This has caused considerable tension and difficulty for some Order members. The view is that we're not allowed to go to other teachers or engage in other practices, that we're essentially prohibited from cross-pollinating with other spiritual traditions and approaches. And yet a considerable number of Order members do it, causing, potentially, strife within themselves and with others in the Order. Is Triratna not mature enough to absorb difference while maintaining its integrity? And given our cultural biases and educational conditioning, is the exploration of other teachings and teachers not essential and inevitable?

SUBHUTI: I don't agree: it's as simple as that, not for our Order and sangha. I think it would be all right if people went to other teachers in the spirit of the Order. So that they made it clear why they were doing it, that they did it in dialogue, and they were very clear about where their loyalties lay. But often people aren't clear about where their loyalties lie, they want their cake and eat it, but I don't think that's fair. There was the case of Anomarati, who became interested in Nyingmapa Buddhism through a retreat at Vajraloka and eventually realised he was a Nyingma, wanted to follow that path and did so, and I thought, great, that's really clear. But it's not often like that.

JYOTIKA: And you think it's unfair because it dilutes our shared understanding?

SUBHUTI: Yes, I think it becomes more difficult to feel in sympathy with each other. This is my whole emphasis. People are obviously free to do what they like but if I am to continue to feel that we are in a sangha together, rather than in a general sangha of all Buddhists, then we need to have a common area of understanding in the fundamental views that we have, the language that we use to describe our experience, and, to some extent, that will depend on us having a shared range of practices. If you've done the Mindfulness of Breathing you know how you work in that practice and that then influences your discourse. For instance, what we're getting with the importation of material from Zen and a kind of neo-Dzogchen and a neo-vipasanna, with little traces of Vedanta, is an alien language, it's a different perspective and I don't think it can graft easily onto what we already have. People could graft it but it will require work, finding out how it fits with what we actually have rather than saying, this is good, this is the best, we should be doing this etc. This creates a lot of conflict, even profound conflict as it brings in questions about what the Order is, so that some may say we don't need devotion or a teacher, and it just becomes a bunch of freelance Buddhists, which is ok but I don't think you can have an Order on that basis. There needs to be some common framework. This is the key issue. Some people don't seem to realise that you can't have the strong sense of shared identity and understanding that you get in the Order if you don't respect the need for a common framework; these things will go.

So, if you do go to other teachers, you need to have a sense of concern for the integrity of the Order, and not wanting to do anything to disturb that, and as you honour your own personal inspiration you do so while honouring Bhante and that from his understanding the Order has unfolded. If you don't have that then you are working out your own disquiets and inspirations, and if you start spreading this then you risk diluting the integrity of the Order.

JYOTIKA: Presumably an Order member's attendance at a talk or retreat led by a teacher from another tradition doesn't mean that their heart is definitely not with the Order?

SUBHUTI: No, no it doesn't.

JYOTIKA: So at what point can it be said that it seems their heart has left?

SUBHUTI: Unfortunately the language of "your heart being with" is entirely subjective. You'd have to start by giving some sort of objective criteria, which is very hard to create. But if somebody started attending such retreats or events then they'd need to be in consultation with critically-minded kalyana mitras, they'd need to be in active dialogue with the Order, with a strong sense that 'I don't want to do anything that harms the Order, I want to be sensitive to it'. Sometimes people think, 'I'm trying something new and it will help the Order' but I think that's less easy than is assumed.

JYOTIKA: There are people who read a lot of different Buddhist authors and gain a lot of inspiration from different books or a particular writer's approach and read everything they have, but it sounds like what you're talking about is if somebody starts to find that their primary source of inspiration is from another teacher or another tradition, and that they are starting to identify themselves and their practice around this tradition or teacher, then it becomes problematic for the integrity of the Order?

SUBHUTI: Yes but I think it can even happen just through reading books. Nobody went on Daniel Ingram's retreats but he had a big influence on some people through his writing. Books can be very influential, especially if people aren't refreshing their understanding of where we come from, and haven't done enough work on integrating Bhante's teachings with their experience.

JYOTIKA: So it becomes problematic if people start teaching the teachings of Buddhist writers who come from other traditions?

SUBHUTI: Yes and it can also become problematic if people start practising in that way too. I wouldn't say that people shouldn't do it but it's important to remember that it will have an effect. You can't go on practising in a way that is different from everybody else and still feel everyone will be ok, especially if your new way of practising undermines our notions of Ordination and devotion or whatever. There are many different ways of practising that come from completely different systems of spiritual discipline. I think there are only a few who are hardheaded and critically minded enough to really see what they're doing once they've started to dip into different systems.

JYOTIKA: So our cohesion, with us operating and practising from a common framework of shared understanding, is extremely important to you?

SUBHUTI: Yes, and not merely as group discipline, I don't want people behaving so that they fit in, but from a sense that their actions, for better or worse, have an impact on their community as a whole. If they don't turn up to events, Order weekends and so forth, if they don't have a Chapter, it has an effect. One needs to be committed to the Order as a practice, which involves usefully subordinating your ego-identity to something bigger. I find it ironic that some of the most individualistic voices are the ones who talk most about getting rid of ego-clinging or selflessness. What you'd expect to see from someone who was selfless was a sense of gratitude for what they've gained and loyalty – which is another word for devotion - to the Order and its origins.

It's a higher demand upon us than most of us realise, certainly it was higher than I'd initially realised. I've had the opportunity to do quite a lot that's affected the Order in a positive way but I've also done things that haven't been so good. This has taught me a certain delicacy in relation to the Order, and I could be more sensitive still.

JYOTIKA: Could you give an example of something you did in which your lack of sensitivity to the Order became apparent?

SUBHUTI: A good example is that I got very excited about Non-Violent Communication (NVC). I don't think I was wrong, I just went about it in a careless way. It would have been better if I'd gone and done a few things myself and maybe got a friend who I knew was critical of these things to come with me. Then we could've discussed it, come up with some sort of report saying why we thought it was a good thing, what the dangers were, highlighting where it came from, what we didn't want from it and so on. And from that basis, we could've made a recommendation of it or not to the College, and then have taken it from there. Whereas I just got enthusiastic about it and started getting people to do it. No great harm done in the long run but there might have been.

JYOTIKA: When did you really see how important and demanding the Order as a 'practice' is?

SUBHUTI: The NVC episode was instructive. Largely it hasn't been a bad thing but I saw a couple of people led astray by it because it sort of comes from a New Agey stable. And some of the background metaphysics is pretty wonky. The founder of NVC, Marshall Rosenberg, had an ex-girlfriend who told me that he is basically a Rabbi, which was a slight caricature but it wasn't completely untrue. So he was starting a new religion. The basics of what he taught – a way of paying attention in communication – is useful, and I still think about it and use it to a degree.

So that was pretty instructive for me. I also think that my own confusions during the early 2000's, while I was Chair of the Public Preceptors' College, helped me, eventually, to see how the responsibilities inherent in engaging with the Order as a practice. I think I did some pretty good things as Chair, like fleshing out the College's position in relation to the Order but I did it in a very clumsy way, which, unfortunately, had an effect. For instance, at that time I spoke publically about the College not being Head of the Order. I was trying to communicate something important with this but I should've used a different rhetoric or language, as how I pitched it broke an archetype. I didn't intend to do this but I didn't have sufficient self-knowledge and this had negative consequences.

Likewise, if you go to another teacher and come back waxing lyrical about them this has an effect. It's not wrong to go, but for the sake of the Order's cohesion you need to do it in a consultative and humble way.

JYOTIKA: You've clearly a very sensitive antenna to the Order's cohesion and how that might be made fragile by the forces around us in society at large.

SUBHUTI: Yes and we're affected by wave upon wave upon wave of powerful influences. Sometimes the extent to which this happens through the Order and movement is almost laughable. Topically, there is the whole question of sexual unskilfulness. And in raising this, I'm not saying that it wasn't a problem in the past, but the style of that, the rhetoric, how it can be spoken of now, is not to do with us, it's from the world around us. Atula told me some time ago that he thought a lot of what we've gone through is from the Trumpeffect; people being generally disillusioned with leaders and a growth in a radicalism, which can, in itself, be destructive.

SYSTEM OF PRACTICE: CLOSING DOWN OR OPENING OUT?

"That's the character of creativity generally; you do your drawings and drawings and drawings and drawings."

Subhuti

JYOTIKA: Some people claim that the *Seven Papers*, as a whole, has established a System of Practice so defined and well-worked out that it is now essentially closed. It was believed that establishing a System of Practice for Triratna would take generations, but doing so now, prematurely, via the *Papers*, will lead to a tightening and weakening of individual spiritual practice and, from there, our collective sclerosis. What's your response to this?

SUBHUTI: I don't agree with this at all. What the *Seven Papers* does is establish a set of basic principles upon which a System of Practice can be formulated. For instance, the schema of the Five Aspects of Spiritual Life is capable of incorporating more or less anything. There is another issue that is more to do with our trying to make sure that we can recognise each other because we share enough common ground. I think that is a separate issue that is not dealt with in the *Papers*. But in terms of them presenting a closed System of Practice, no, I don't agree at all. I'm surprised anyone should see it like that.

JYOTIKA: The issue of how we recognise each other, is *A Buddhist Manifesto* not an attempt to articulate that?

SUBHUTI: Yes but again that's mainly about principles.

JYOTIKA: As opposed to …

SUBHUTI: Saying, for example, that you must do the Mindfulness of Breathing, that these are the practices you must conform to. The *Seven Papers,* instead, give a basis for continuing evolution. Without such an exposition of Bhante's fundamental position, everybody makes it up for themselves. When people start making it up for themselves a sense of alienation increases between those who have done that and others who don't recognise the way they're talking. For me, a fundamental moment was when somebody started talking to me about the 'seven jnanas' and I realised that I'd no idea what they were talking about. This is because it's not part of our common basic vocabulary; it's from Daniel Ingram. For some people he became an authority, and that alerted me to the dangers that here was someone whose work was being used in some Centres and on some retreats but without any reference to, or integration with, a commonly agreed framework, and so it could be very hard to follow what people were talking about. If you made the effort, you could figure it out, but there was something about the language that was alien.

So I think there needs to be a commonly shared framework of understanding, and the *Papers* tries to set this out. The paper on *An Initiation into a New Life* ties together metaphysical doctrine, the emphasis on Going for Refuge, the understanding of a System of Practice, and our Ordination ceremony so that you can see it all as a whole, which for many people was a great relief. Recently I led a retreat with people from different Buddhist sanghas. I know a fair bit about Buddhist history and philosophy so when we had a collective discussion I'd a reasonable idea of where each was coming from but there was such distance between them that the discussion became abstract very easily. I think if the Order loses our shared framework of understanding, it will lose a huge amount of potency. It will be very difficult to have a system of linked Centres or a system of training for Ordination linked to Centres because at Padmaloka you'll have to deal with people who've been sitting facing a wall contemplating koans and others who've received Tantric transmissions, so that communication would become increasingly abstract; you'd be having to work your way into what they are saying, you might have some sense of kinship but to go deeper than that there needs be a shared language.

I led a study group on the Dharma Section of *The Three Jewels* on the first Tuscany retreat I was on. In this, Bhante talks about the need for a specific system of spiritual discipline. I found this a very telling phrase and it clarified to me why we are different and why we can't just accept anybody. The discourse of individuality, and some people's loss of faith because of issues from the past, contributed to us losing focus on this, so it wasn't until 2009 that we finally began to get clarity.

JYOTIKA: Isiah Berlin said that, "Spontaneity is compatible with self-surrender but not with system" meaning, I think, that a system is boundaried, and boundaries and limits prohibit spontaneity, whereas when you surrender to 'other' you give up control and identification with boundaries, and that this renunciation allows spontaneity to emerge: this seems contrary to what you're saying about the need for 'system' and 'discipline'.

SUBHUTI: I don't know if I agree with Berlin's statement, there are so many ill-defined terms. What occurs to me, for instance, is when you meditate you start off with a practice and it has a form, a system if you like, it has boundaries but if you do it with a degree of intelligence and sensitivity it begins to take on a life of its own. I would say that system and form are the basis of creativity (I'm not sure what spontaneity means). That's the character of creativity generally; you do your drawings and drawings and drawings and drawings.

JYOTIKA: The discipline of the craft.

SUBHUTI: Yes. The Berlin quote sounds like a false dichotomy. I'm sure he's far too intelligent to mean something so crude but that's how it reads. I believe that 'form' is underestimated – you need a structure, a system, a form, but it must be informed by inspiration, as well as allowing and permitting fresh inspiration. That fresh inspiration doesn't necessarily have to be something new and original; you might keep doing the same old practice but a new spirit might have entered into it.

And this is part of our, Triratna's, understanding of practice with form: samaya sattva and jnana sattva – you use the conventional image and that becomes informed by the creative image.

We need a system that is always related to principle and that is capable of renewal, correction, adaptation, development, and one where if and when we ask, "why are we doing this?" somebody knows! That it's not simply being done for the sake of it. It should always be possible to say, "what's the purpose of this? What's its meaning? What are we trying to get from it?"

JYOTIKA: The paper, *Reimagining the Buddha*, looks explicitly at the issues of creativity and Imagination. Do any of the other papers touch on or explore this idea that creativity, or innovation, can and will emerge from a practice, a system, a discipline?

SUBHUTI: *Revering and Relying upon the Dharma* looks at the Five Niyamas. The Dhamma niyama is the creative force, and this force arises because you have previously created the conditions for it. The background language to an *Initiation into a New Life* is that of the niyamas, in fact the language of the *Papers* is the language of the niyamas. And the *Supra-personal Force* is all about creativity.

But how do you plunge into creativity? I remember being oppressed by this idea: I must be myself, I must create from within myself. But how do you do that? It's not something you self-consciously do. If you set out to be creative and innovate you'll only produce 'fancy', in Coleridge's terms, rather than imagination. So much of modern art is like that, someone doing something clever that nobody's thought of before. Sometimes it is very interesting but that doesn't necessarily make it creative.

In the *Papers*, the Dhamma niyama is the creative force par excellence, which works on lesser levels; Bhante has hinted that it functions within the other niyamas to lift them up but that's getting too speculative.

JYOTIKA: To follow on from this, Bhante also said in *What is the Western Buddhist Order?* that, "there should not be innovation in terms of principles" and "there is less creativity or originality now [*than there was in the early days*] because so much of the work has already been done and needs to be developed rather than originated."

Obviously, the *early days* can never be repeated, but perhaps this last statement is debateable, inasmuch as we may, in the future, as a community, go through another period of widespread creative flourishing, marked, as the early days were, by fervent activity, experimentation and idealism. From this, is there a case to be made that we've had almost ten years of conservation, of systematization based on clear principles, and that a much greater focus and direction of resources needs now to go into creativity and innovation, be that through the encouragement of Order members to start new Centres, businesses, sustainable communities etc and/or through artistic, intellectual and educational pursuits?

SUBHUTI: Again, I'd put the case that what we've been doing is clarifying the form, based on principle. Bhante's quote conflates creativity and originality, but they are not necessarily the same thing. By saying there is less originality, he is saying that the Order is basically set up. It will continue to develop from here but we're no longer in the phase of starting something new. I think that's all he's saying.

Over the last few years, I think we've been trying to recover from un-resolved issues in our conduct in the past, some of our ideas in the past and certain principles that were not made sufficiently clear in the past. Since 2009 we've made things much clearer and more explicit. And my sense is that there has been a surge of new energy, especially from focusing on young people. That had become a problem pre-2009, we'd stopped attracting young people. The fascinating thing is that young people value the structures more than the old lags as it gives them a form, a discernible path, for their lives.

So the right form, with the right attitude to it, leads to creativity.

JYOTIKA: What is the right attitude?

SUBHUTI: Well, venerating it because of what it gives you, remembering why you are doing it and being concerned with keeping it vital and alive. I don't think you can have an *emphasis* on creativity: it's either there or it's not. It seems to me that clarity releases energy, which is essential for creativity.

FINAL QUESTIONS

JYOTIKA: Why were the discussions you had with Bhante that led to the *Seven Papers* one of the highlights of your life?

SUBHUTI: They were one of the highlights of my life because I felt we were both very fully engaged in an extremely creative process of drawing out the deeper implications of the Dhamma. It was deeply satisfying and fulfilling both intellectually and spiritually, and left me personally transformed by a new dimension of understanding. I can't expect anybody reading the *Papers* now to have the same experience but that is how it was for me. It was among the most complete and satisfying communications of my life.

JYOTIKA: And more generally, within your life, how has Bhante's guidance led to greater spiritual depth?

SUBHUTI: One of the questions you asked was something like, is my approach predominantly rational. It's not. I'm a faith-type, though I hope an intelligent one. I've been driven by a strong discomfort with the world as it was presented to me and a very deep attraction to the Dhamma as it was presented by Bhante. The vision that Bhante unfolded affected me very deeply and it's driven me all the time. I've a moderately trained mind, with a moderate intelligence and I like things to add up and make sense, where possible. "To fathom the fathomable, and quietly revere the unfathomable." As Goethe says. And I'm capable of revering. But unclarity bothers me. If I don't understand I feel uncomfortable because I think a lack of understanding can lead to the wrong path. Probably that has sometimes led me into over-rationalisation – I don't deny that – but I think often it's led me to greater and greater clarity. But the clarity that I get I don't see as a pre-dominantly intellectual one. Through thinking clearly about the Dhamma, and

Bhante has very much encouraged this, I can get to a point where thinking stops and there is just pure experience, which I call *conviction*. This isn't a holding a postulate in the mind, it's that I've passed beyond the intellect to a direct experience. Bhante has, again and again, led me to this experience of transcending myself. This has happened largely through his extraordinary clarity of exposition. I've also been deeply attracted to his presentation of myth: the Tantric Path, White Lotus Sutra and Sutra of Golden Light Series were all highly formative for me. The sadhana practices that he's given me have been the basis of my spiritual life. Bhante's both initiated me into them and given me an understanding of what I'm doing and, as I've said, if I don't know what I'm doing I feel very uneasy, it's like a kind of intellectual dukkha – if things are unclear maybe they're erroneous.

JYOTIKA: This experience of *conviction*, has that deepened over the years?

SUBHUTI: In a certain sense it hasn't – when you see, you see – but I experience it now with greater ease and it's more present to me more of the time, so, because of that, it's a richer experience.

JYOTIKA: A big part of your practice has been with the creation, maintenance and development of sangha, so has this – has kalyana mitrata – been a way into this experience?

SUBHUTI: Well, I'm a man of practical energy and Bhante gave me a vision that I could serve practically, and I'm enormously grateful to him for it. Initially, I was happy scraping walls and hammering nails but then I got involved in building sangha because you can't separate them out. And with great naivety, I did my best. My relationship with others has led to huge personal changes – changes that wouldn't have been possible without them. How much progress I've made because of this is not for me to say, but my sympathies have got much broader over the years, and I can now relate positively and more deeply to a far greater range of personalities and types. I've also been in leadership positions over the years, and I believe I'm much better at it now: I don't have to lead from the front as I used to, I can bring people with me, and I'm more self-critical and can take criticism much better.

JYOTIKA: In terms of transformation, has more happened via meditation, study, reflection – the contemplative practices – or via sangha building, deepening friendships, realising you've hurt people, forgiving etc?

SUBHUTI: It's hard to say, it's been all of a bundle. I don't think I can isolate any particular aspect when looking at my spiritual development. This is a concern I have in relation to ways that Insight is sometimes discussed. The way it's sometimes spoken or written about, gives a very narrow perspective on spiritual life; it can be an important perspective but also very narrow.

I'm sure I've much further to go but I know I'm wiser and much more mature than I was, and that's because of the total context of our community. That includes, of course, the difficulties and the mistakes, of which I've made many.

So I'm profoundly grateful for the context I've had: the movement as a practice and as a community, with my many friends and some antagonists, who have been extremely useful to me, of course, as I've had to come to terms with them too.

JYOTIKA: Ok, that's it from me. Thanks so much for taking the time to answer my questions.

INDEX

Dates

A

B

C

D

E

F

G

H

NOTES